Myths & Folktales of the Alabama-Coushatta Indians of Texas

MYTHS & FOLKTALES OF THE ALABAMA-COUSHATTA INDIANS OF TEXAS By Howard N. Martin

THE ENCINO PRESS   AUSTIN

To Valerie

©1977 : Howard N. Martin
I.S.B.N. 0-88426-052-6

Woodcut illustration by Barbara Mathews Whitehead

Foreword

TWENTY THOUSAND years before his arrival in East Texas, the ances-
tral Indian had lived in Asia. This ancestor to the Battises, Bullocks,
Sylestines, and Ponchos—all the Alabamas and Coushattas—was a hunter
and a gatherer. He lived on the edge of game herds, moving with them,
stampeding them, running down the cripples, and hurling his spear into
their paunches so that eventually he could finish them off with rocks
and clubs. He hunted the mastodon and the mammoth, musk oxen and
horses. He used fire and he dressed in skins to keep out the aching gla-
cial cold. His cheek bones were high; his eyes had the slant; and his lids
had the fold that typified his people.

Then one morning the Old Chief saw the herds moving north and
eastward. He assembled the tribe, who to themselves were The People,
and together they began their trek beyond memory out of Asia, north
to the Bering Isthmus, then across to Alaska. They spent a winter in a
long valley where the caribou and the musk ox broke through the ice
and snow for the fodder and foliage that lay beneath, and when spring
came they moved again, this time to the south.

The women and children gathered wild berries and roots and plants,
and the men hunted. Hunt and gather; starve and stuff. They stopped
by a river for the summer months and fattened themselves on the sal-
mon that journeyed to the final shallows to spawn and die. They ate
the big blueberries that grew on the tundra and the sweet little straw-
berries that grew on the sand spits near the water. And they ate the
great brown bears that ate the berries and the fish, and they ate the
fish roe that they found jellied together in the quiet water, and they
ate the hellgrammites and the swift trout that ate the roe.

The game moved and generations of The People moved out of Alaska
and down the long trench of the Columbia River that flowed to the
warmer regions to the south. They met Strangers and fought with some
and banded with others. Fat kine and lean; birth and burial; winter, but
always followed by spring and rebirth of The People and game and the
Earth's yield. They flourished and became a tribe. And the bison gave
way to the buffalo, and the earth warmed for them, and The People
hunted the deer and antelope.

Always they moved to the south. South along the eastern flank of
the Rockies, edging toward the great herds of the plains. South, learn-

ing the use of the atlatl and the bola and the bow. South, chipping the flint and weaving a few crude baskets and patting and rolling clay into the form of pots. South along the Sierra Madre Oriental, over the Mexican plains and the gentle hills, across canyons and crags, through the rain forests, over the High Plain of the Sun, into the jungles of Yucatan they moved. They moved so slowly that it surprised them to remember where they came from, and the stories the Old Ones told around the fire were of a strange and ancient past in another world.

Sometimes they moved to keep up with the movement of game or to find better fields to gather in. Sometimes, and this was often, they were pushed by fiercer, stronger tribes following them from the north and close on their heels. And The People could remember moving just to move.

The Yucatan Peninsula stopped their journey only for a while, for the sea was but a brief barrier. Some of The People stayed behind, but many followed the wind and currents of the Caribbean northward from one island to another until they landed on the American Gulf Coast and began new lives and continued old lives in Florida and Georgia and Alabama.

But there were always pressures and movement. Other people had already come to the new land and had rested and planted and built their temple-topped mounds and had moved on restlessly. Now The Tribe felt the pressure from a stronger and an alien people with different skins and different clothes pouring down and across from the north and east, and they began a movement again, following old trails to the west. Two generations later they came to their last home in the pine hills of East Texas. Those who preceded them, the Caddos to the north and the Atakapans to the south, were already disappearing, their final homes being their burial ground. The People—the Alabamas and Coushattas—would bury many of their own before they could claim their Polk County hunting ground.

Howard Martin collected during a time when the tales were still alive in the minds of some of the Old Ones. Sometimes the stories were told among themselves or brought out of a dim past to tell to a grandchild, but mostly they were old recollections in old memories, the things past of such tribesmen as Chief Charles Martin Thompson, McConico Battise, Bronson Cooper Sylestine, and Charles Boatman, who had grown up with the stories in their traditions and real lives fifty and sixty years earlier. Since that time, the missionaries had come with new myths and

Foreword

new tales, and museum collectors had come and hauled off their past and their artifacts by the wagonload. And there was always a struggle to survive intact in a white man's culture which often looked on their alien ways without sympathy.

The tales had lain dormant for a long time before Howard Martin resurrected them in the 1930s, and by the time he got out of the Navy in 1946, nearly all the Old Ones had died and taken the memory of those old ways and words with them. It is most ironical that when the Alabama-Coushatta got into the tourist business in 1970 they had to go to the Indians of Oklahoma for a refresher course in the old ways of singing and dancing and dressing.

The Old Ones remembered stories told before the missionaries came, stories of their tribes' own special creation and stories of the beginnings of things of their own culture—of tobacco and language and corn— stories of The People when the Indians and the gods and the animals all walked the hunting grounds together and talked together. The Old Ones told the tales, knowing in their imaginations what the gods looked like and how they appareled themselves when they appeared to men. They knew Rabbit and Fox and Bear as men know them totemically and as forms of life that lived in the forest world much as the Indian did, with the same fears and the same problems. The old tellers of tales knew intimately the witches and demons and Man-Eaters, phantasms who were as real as their most personal fears and as real as the red oak trees and the cold north wind that blew through their cabins' cracks.

These tales seem strange to us, some of them. Sometimes they come out unmotivated or incomplete—but that is our lack, not theirs. Between them and us is a gap in time and space and a wide gap between cultures and conditioning. The myths that we are acquainted with are those of the Greeks and the Romans and the myths of the Hebrews, and our talking animals come from the world of Uncle Remus and Walt Disney. The classical myths are easy for us to understand because they have been a part of an enduring western culture for over two thousand years and because they were written down by professional and accomplished storytellers, by Homer and Hesiod and Virgil and Ovid. They are well-constructed stories that have been told and written so many times that they have grown into complete literary forms.

The Old Testament stories of the Hebrews are much closer in structure to the Alabama-Coushatta myths because they were trapped and written down in a primitive time, and as with the Indian tales, much of the filler—the explanation of character and motivation—is left out. Just as the Indians knew what was between the lines, so did the Hebrews. When the tales were alive and circulating the Hebrews knew where Adam's sons got their wives and what the mark of Cain was and why Noah cursed Ham just for seeing him naked. Moderns sometimes read and wonder.

We wonder too as we read these Alabama-Coushatta tales about how the old woman got the sun in a pot in the first place, or why a cold bath keeps one healthy, or what the horned owl-crawfish represents. But even as we wonder, we remember that we are reading the notes to a song, not hearing it sung. We regret that we have not an Indian *scop*, a shaper of words and sounds, to tell these tales to us in all their earthly and unearthly dimensions, to thrill us with the action of battle or the hunt or to chill our hearts as we imagine awakening at night in the deep woods to see a ghostly, glowing raccoon standing just beyond the fire-light's ring, looking at us.

The teller is all. His personality, the look in his eye, the movement of his hands and body, the sounds of his voice: these things are the life of a story and they are the tools that the teller uses to build with. He is a creative artist, molding his characters into many dimensions, breathing life into them out of the experience of his own life—creating new worlds out of old ones and worlds above it and below it—and finally bringing these things and all that man grapples with into an understandable pattern and order. This last is the ultimate value of the teller and the tale, to bring into some comprehensible order the adventures of a culture, to take the random-scattered tales of the Alabama and Coushatta Indians and to help the reader see them and understand them in their own tribe's perspective.

The tellers are all gone now—the Old Ones sleep beneath the sand—but the mind's eye can work magic with a word.

Francis Edward Abernethy
Stephen F. Austin State University
Nacogdoches, Texas

Preface

THE Alabamas and Coushattas have resided in the Big Thicket region of Southeast Texas continuously since the 1780s. Some 600 of the tribe's current 680 members live on the Alabama-Coushatta Indian Reservation.

The tales in this volume typify the verbal tradition of these two tribes. The essential forms of most of these stories, both the ones that seem several centuries old and those that hint at contact with European settlers, had become firmly set by the time of their last westward migration—in the 1760s—on a route from Alabama through Louisiana to Texas.

During the decade of the 1780s small groups of both tribes began moving across the Sabine River into Spanish Texas. They occupied areas of the Big Thicket, which provided them a subsistence source and a refuge. Since 1854 these Indians have lived on a reservation in Polk County, Texas. They have managed to remain in their Polk County homes when all the other Texas tribes (except the Tiguas, near El Paso) were either exterminated or driven outside the state's borders.

Beginning in 1931, I have made a special study of the Alabama and Coushatta Tribes of Indians. I was born and raised in Livingston, Texas, seventeen miles from the present Alabama-Coushatta Indian Reservation, and my contacts with these people began with boyhood associations with members of these two tribes.

Many early reports prepared as writing assignments for high school and college courses, plus later materials prepared for historical and folklore journals, expanded my investigative efforts into an ever-deepening and more determined search not only for general, but also for primary, materials relating specifically to these two tribes. Over the years I have interviewed many members of these two tribes and other people who, by long association with them, have become part of their history. Also, I have searched for historical and cultural materials about these Indians in various archives and other records depositories, utilizing every reference source available.

I began systematically collecting Alabama-Coushatta myths and folktales in 1931, and most of this work was completed during the subsequent ten-year period. I interviewed numerous residents on the Polk County reservation, but only nineteen of the older men and women were found to be useful informants. Very few of the younger Indians knew any of the stories.

First and foremost among the Alabama-Coushatta storytellers was Charles Martin Thompson. He was an expert woodworker, especially in producing bows, arrows, and flutes. When John R. Swanton, an ethnologist from the Bureau of American Ethnology, visited the Alabama-Coushatta Reservation in 1911 and 1912, Thompson (or Sun-Ke) served as his translator for interviews with the Polk County Indians. Two decades later, on December 21-22, 1932, he recorded numerous songs and described eleven dances for Frances Densmore, a field representative of the Bureau of American Ethnology. He was a faithful member of the Presbyterian Mission Church on the reservation and served his church as a deacon. In 1928, at the age of 67, he was elected chief of his tribe. Accompanied by Speaker Chief McConico Battise and Second Chief Clem Fain, Jr., Chief Thompson journeyed to Washington, D.C., to request assistance for the Polk County Indians. As a result, the reservation was substantially enlarged. He continued to serve as tribal chief until his death in September, 1935.

Next in order is McConico Battise, the Speaker Chief and father of the present chief, Fulton Battise. He was one of the oldest and wisest of the Alabamas. A leader in the Presbyterian Mission Church throughout his adult life, he was prominent in all reservation activities. He was a valuable source of information about Alabama-Coushatta folklore, and his assistance in recording stories in this collection and preparing the narratives in final form is gratefully acknowledged.

The third principal storyteller was Bronson Cooper Sylestine, nephew of Charles Martin Thompson and great-grandson of an early-nineteenth-century leader of the Alabamas. He was a large man—6'3'' tall—and was 89 years old at his death in 1969. He was first a deacon and later an elder in the Presbyterian Mission Church. On January 1, 1936, in an elaborate curtain-raiser for the Texas Centennial, he was installed as chief of the Alabama-Coushattas. In addition to receiving the tribal chief's paraphernalia on this occasion, he was presented a special medal by order of the Texas Legislature.

Other principal informants include Charles Boatman, a Coushatta and an expert in dances and music as well as folktales; Billy Harrison Battise; Frank Sylestine; and Gustin Battise.

To my primary group of myths and folktales collected through personal interviews, I added stories from other collectors of Alabama-Coushatta narratives. Those who permitted me to use their materials include two members of the Alabama tribe: James L. D. Sylestine, Sgt.,

U.S. Army, son of the late Chief Bronson Cooper Sylestine, who attended Austin College (Sherman, Texas) and Austin Presbyterian Theological Seminary; and Matthew Bullock, an outstanding athlete in football, basketball, and track, who graduated from Austin College with a B.A. degree in mathematics, and recently retired after 22 years of service as an engineer with the Texas Department of Highways and Public Transportation. The third folklore collector whose assistance I wish to acknowledge is Clem Fain, Jr., a Livingston attorney who was appointed state agent for the Polk County Indians in 1928. Elected an honorary member and second chief of the combined Alabama and Coushatta tribes, he organized the successful trip to Washington, D.C., in 1928, which sought enlargement of the Alabama-Coushatta reservation. He later served as a member of the Texas Senate.

When I began my interviews among the Alabamas and Coushattas, I found that generally these Indians were reluctant to discuss their folklore. Some claimed they had forgotten the stories, while others apparently did not like to talk about such matters with anyone except a fellow tribesman. For many of my folklore-gathering trips, therefore, I enlisted the assistance of Matthew Bullock, one of my teammates on high school and junior college football teams. He accompanied me on visits to various people on the reservation and served as translator. Most of the Indians whom we visited were willing to tell the stories in their own language to Matthew, who would then translate each story into English, as I took notes. Also, I wish to acknowledge the assistance of the late Dr. and Mrs. C. W. Chambers, who served as missionaries on the Alabama-Coushatta Reservation from 1899 to 1937 and who encouraged the Indians to talk about their folklore.

I collected at least five—and occasionally as many as ten—versions of each Alabama-Coushatta narrative. Some informants related parts of a story that others omitted. There were differences in the organization of motifs within stories, and motifs were interchanged freely. Many variations in descriptions of story characters and action also occurred.

Since the Alabamas and Coushattas have lived in contiguous culture areas for so many years, their myths and folktales have blended to the extent that my Indian informants could not label some stories as "Alabama" and others "Coushatta." They pointed out that a story related by a member of one tribe might have been borrowed from a member of the other tribe—or from members of other nearby tribes.

After gathering notes on the folklore of these two tribes, I wrote a consensus version of each story, assisted by Charles Martin Thompson, McConico Battise, and Bronson Cooper Sylestine—all members of the Alabama tribe. Thus every story in my collection is presented in the form in which it was generally known among the most reliable story-tellers on the Alabama-Coushatta Reservation during the 1931-1940 period. Some of these myths and folktales appeared in a paperback edition which I published in 1946. For the present edition, I selected 46 stories which represent both the most common and the most intriguing examples of the Alabama-Coushatta narratives.

Major sources of information for any study relating to Indians of the southeastern United States—including Alabamas and Coushattas—are the articles, books, and Bureau of American Ethnology archival material credited to John R. Swanton. I never met this noted ethnologist, but I corresponded with him while I was a student at the University of Texas at Austin during 1937-1941. He informed me that he had visited the Alabama-Coushatta Reservation in 1911 and 1912, but that his visits were so brief he had time to obtain stories from only three people— Celissy Henry, George Henry, and Charles Martin Thompson. He expressed interest in my efforts to collect additional stories from the Alabamas and Coushattas and emphasized the importance of two efforts: contacting as many of these people as possible—especially the older men and women—and obtaining the maximum number of variants of each story. These suggestions guided my subsequent activity in Alabama-Coushatta folklore collection—which, in its entirety, constitutes a continuation of the project initiated by Dr. Swanton 20 years earlier.

It simply is not possible to acknowledge fully the numerous individuals whose aid and encouragement over many years have made this publication possible. I do wish, however, to express special appreciation to a few persons, in addition to those already mentioned in this preface, whose direct or indirect influence on the development of this volume has been prominent.

The instruction and counsel of two English teachers early in my formal education continue to influence my investigative and reporting activities: Ruth Pritchard, Livingston High School; and Donnella Smith, Lon Morris College, Jacksonville, Texas.

At the University of Texas at Austin I was a student in classes taught by Eugene C. Barker and J. Frank Dobie. Dr. Barker stressed the importance of "digging deeper" for historical facts, an impression that has guided all of my subsequent research activities. Professor Dobie underscored the urgency to accelerate my folklore collecting while the older Polk County Indians in the 1930s were still alive. As the result of numerous conferences with Dr. Mody C. Boatright, I prepared a manuscript containing a limited selection of Alabama-Coushatta stories which was published in 1946.

It is a pleasure, also, to acknowledge my indebtedness to Dr. Francis E. Abernethy, Professor of English at Stephen F. Austin State University and Secretary-Editor of the Texas Folklore Society, for his kindness in reading the proof and consenting to write the foreword.

The interest and cooperation of a number of people with Alabama-Coushatta governmental and administrative responsibilities have been demonstrated on numerous occasions, and I wish to express sincere appreciation to Chief Fulton Battise, Second Chief Emmett Battise (who serves also as reservation superintendent), the Alabama-Coushatta Tribal Council under the chairmanship of Clayton Sylestine, and Walter Broemer, Executive Director of the Texas Indian Commission.

My special thanks are due to Charles A. Kasdorf, III, who read the entire manuscript with painstaking care, provided a lengthy and incisive set of comments for improving its contents, and shared the tedious tasks of indexing and proofreading. Also, I wish to acknowledge the contributions of various typists and proofreaders who helped to prepare the manuscript for publication, including Katherine Slocum, Lillian Engel, Lynette Hartwick, and Yolanda Cazares.

My family bore patiently the pressures caused by my commitment to complete this book. My wife, Valerie, has been a source of constant encouragement. Without her this book could never have been written.

Howard N. Martin
Houston, Texas
May 25, 1976

Contents

Introduction

HISTORICAL BACKGROUND

The Alabamas and Coushattas are separate tribes, but have been
closely related throughout their history. Both of Muskhogean stock,
they lived in adjoining areas of Alabama, followed similar migration
routes westward, and settled in the same area of the Southeast Texas
Big Thicket. Culturally these two tribes have always been one people, in
spite of minor differences: their languages are mutually understandable,
and their ties have been continuously renewed through intermarriage,
which has been the rule since earliest times.

Alabamas and Coushattas were members of the Upper Creek Confederacy, an organization built around a group of dominant tribes called
Muskogee and located primarily in the present state of Alabama. A cardinal objective of the Creek Confederacy was to achieve a defensive
alliance against common enemies, among whom were the English
settlers along the Atlantic Coast and the Choctaw Indians in the territory that included Mississippi and parts of Alabama and Louisiana.

The name "Alabama" is derived from a combination of words meaning "vegetation gatherers." "Coushatta" is a popular form of "Koasati,"
which probably contains the words for "cane," "reed," or "white
cane."

EARLY EUROPEAN CONTACTS: The first written references to
the Alabamas, dated 1541, relate the contacts of the explorer Hernando
De Soto with these Indians, probably within what is now Mississippi.
After De Soto, the Alabamas are lost to view until the appearance of
the French in the region bordering the Gulf of Mexico. The Alabamas,
who had migrated eastward during the intervening one and a half centuries, then lived near the junction of the Coosa and Tallapoosa Rivers,
the two main tributaries of the Alabama River.

While the French were establishing themselves at Mobile, they became involved in skirmishes with the Alabama and Mobile tribes. Peace
was soon restored, however, and thereafter the French and the Alabamas remained good friends. This friendship was cemented in 1714 by
the founding of Fort Toulouse in the heart of the Alabamas' homeland
near the current site of Montgomery.

WESTWARD MIGRATION: In 1763 the struggle between England

and France for supremacy in North America ended, and control of French-held territory passed to the English. When the English arrived in the Alabama River region to establish their administrative framework, substantial numbers of the Indians in that area moved westward, having been convinced by the French that the English were their enemies.

Many of the Alabamas and Coushattas who lived around Fort Toulouse migrated in 1763 from their homes on the Alabama River to southern Louisiana, probably traveling by water to avoid the land of the Choctaws, their enemies in western Alabama, Mississippi, and eastern Louisiana. Small groups of Alabamas settled along the Red River and elsewhere in Louisiana, but their principal settlement was near Opelousas. The Coushattas also established several villages, the largest of which was on the Sabine River about eighty miles south of Natchitoches.

SETTLEMENT IN SPANISH TEXAS: In the 1780s—within two decades of starting their westward migration—the Alabamas and Coushattas began drifting across the border into Spanish Texas. Here they were welcomed by the Spanish officials, who expected them to strengthen the cordon of friendly tribes on Texas' eastern border, which stood guard against first the French and then, after 1803, the Americans. The Spanish knew maintenance of this defense line depended substantially on the loyal service of the Indians; their own garrisons between the Trinity and Sabine Rivers were merely a token presence. The Spanish had to engage in a tug-of-war with the Americans for the Indians' loyalty, and the Indians capitalized on this situation, proffering friendship to both sides in exchange for gifts of clothing, medals, knives, guns, and similar items.

During the early nineteenth century, the Coushattas blazed a vital trail from the Sabine River west to La Bahia. This trail, the Coushatta Trace, became a wilderness thoroughfare for Indians, smugglers, and adventurers traveling between Mexico and Louisiana. Coushattas were posted at strategic points, both on the Coushatta Trace and along the Trinity River, to inform the Spanish in Nacogdoches of any movement— an effort to control illegal or undesirable traffic through the heart of East Texas.

Alabama settlement was occurring slightly to the north of the Coushattas. By 1805, the Alabamas had established a village on the Angelina River and had built homes along Attoyac Bayou and the Neches River. In 1809 the combined population of Alabamas and Coushattas within seventy miles of Nacogdoches was about 1,650.

By 1830, Alabamas were clustered in three communities in north-western Tyler County, and Coushatta villages had reached their zenith near the Trinity River on sites in present Polk County and San Jacinto County, some forty miles southwest. These villages, typical of Alabama and Coushatta towns, consisted of a core area and a succession of neighborhoods scattered through the woods and connected by a network of trails.

Peachtree Village, the largest and most prominent of the Alabama communities, was the northern terminus of Long King's Trace, and through it passed the Alabama Trace and the Coushatta Trace. Five miles southeast, on the Liberty-Nacogdoches Road, lay Fenced-In Village, second in importance. The third Alabama community, Cane Island Village, was located between Peachtree Village and Fort Teran on the Neches River.

In or near the three Coushatta villages lived some 600 members of the tribe in 1830. The Upper Coushatta Village, or Battise Village, was propitiously located where the Coushatta Trace crossed the Trinity River. Long King's Village, the Middle Coushatta Village, was the most prominent of the three, however: here lived Long King, mingo (or chief) above all other Coushatta chiefs. In the Lower Coushatta Village lived Colita, Long King's successor, who became one of the best-known Indian leaders in East Texas.

The Alabama and Coushatta villages were based on farming and hunting. Their location on various traces, some of which were heavily traveled, permitted frequent trade with white settlers.

UNDER THE REPUBLIC OF TEXAS: At General Sam Houston's request, the Alabamas and Coushattas remained neutral in Texas' War for Independence. A few of the Alabamas moved to the Opelousas district of Louisiana until the end of the war. The Coushattas and the remaining Alabamas did not observe strict neutrality, however: in 1836, prior to the Battle of San Jacinto, they fed and cared for white settlers fleeing Santa Anna's advancing army.

In succeeding years, white settlers began to encroach on land occupied by the Alabamas and Coushattas, and actions by the Congress of the Republic of Texas did not ameliorate the problem.

The year 1840 found the Coushattas on the move: as white settlers claimed their village sites, village life began to disintegrate. Prospects brightened briefly when the Congress in 1840 granted two leagues of land—one including Battise Village, the other including Colita's Village—

to the Coushattas for permanent reservations. The land was surveyed and the field notes were filed, but the grants never became effective: white settlers already had claimed the land. Colonel Hamilton Washington subsequently purchased Colita's village site and permitted the Coushattas to remain.

In 1840 the Congress also granted to the Alabamas two leagues of land which included Fenced-In Village. Again the good intentions of the Republic were thwarted: when surveyors came to survey the grant, the Alabamas, thinking the grant was for white settlers, departed for other homesites, leaving their hogs, cattle, and 200 acres of fenced arable land. They drifted southward and formed a village near the confluence of Big and Little Cypress Creeks.

END OF MIGRATION: For nearly a decade after the Republic of Texas became the twenty-eighth state in 1845, the Alabamas and Coushattas fared little better. The Alabama village site was purchased in 1852 by James Barclay, who later became a state agent for the Alabamas, and was known as Jim Barclay Village. Next the Alabamas lived briefly at a site on Woods Creek in eastern Polk County called Rock Village. In 1854 the State of Texas purchased 1,110.7 acres of heavily timbered land in Polk County as a reservation for the Alabamas, and about 500 members of the tribe settled there during the winter of 1854-1855.

During this period, the Coushattas displaced from Long King's Village and Battise Village were compelled to wander around Polk County forests or join those remaining at Colita's Village on Colonel Washington's plantation. Coushatta prospects grew dimmer with the death in 1852 of Chief Colita, who had given the tribe such effective leadership that the *Galveston News* editorially lamented his passing.

In 1855, a year after purchasing the land for the Alabama reservation, the Texas legislature granted the Coushattas 640 acres of land as a permanent home. Suitable open land no longer was available in Polk County, however, and this grant remained only a scrap of paper. Four years later—with the permission of their kinsmen, the Alabamas— approximately 250 Coushattas settled on the Alabama reservation. A few remained on the Hamilton Washington plantation in San Jacinto County until 1906, when they joined the others in Polk County.

During the Civil War, the Polk County Indians served for brief periods in three branches of the Confederate military—infantry, cavalry, and navy. Governors Francis R. Lubbock and Pendleton Murrah commented favorably on their loyal service, and the state legislature provided funds for a salary of an agent for these Indians during 1861-1865.

THE DARK DAYS 1866-1879: The thirty-year period preceding the establishment of the Republic of Texas was the high point in the early history of the Polk County Indian tribes: their friendship was sought first by the Spanish, then by the Mexicans, and finally by American settlers moving into Texas.

The decline began soon after the Battle of San Jacinto in 1836 and reached the low point during the fourteen-year period following the Civil War. After 1865 the Indians had a home, but little else. Few could speak English effectively, and few could find jobs. The state government, concerned mainly with problems of the Reconstruction, provided no real assistance. Official neglect probably mirrored private antipathy: bitter fighting between settlers and such warlike tribes as the Apache, Comanche, and Sioux bred a widespread belief that most Indians were bad, and it was difficult to arouse public sympathy for the peaceful Polk County Indians.

The commandant of the federal Military Post of Livingston (Texas) in 1870 made a report in which he stated that the Polk County Indians needed an agent for their protection, and he volunteered to serve in this capacity until other arrangements could be made. The national government did not respond to this suggestion. In 1872, the state government appointed an agent, but his appointment was not renewed, and the Polk County Indians had no other agent until 1928.

The influx of white settlers into the Big Thicket during the 1870s, the clearing of forests, and the plowing of farmlands nearly destroyed the hunting and fishing practices of the Polk County Indians. They were forced either to rely primarily on farming their limited, worn-out reservation lands or to seek employment outside the reservation boundaries. The lowest point came in 1879, when the state abolished the post of agent for the Polk County Indians.

BEGINNING OF A NEW DAWN 1880-1910: After 1880 the picture began to brighten. This period was marked by three factors that exerted a vast influence on the Alabamas and Coushattas.

The first was construction of a Houston-Shreveport railroad which passed through Polk County. The railroad, which reached Polk County in 1881, opened the gate for development of the logging and lumber industry, which provided job opportunities and steady cash incomes to many Indian families for the first time.

The second, and even more important, influence was the coming of Christianity and education. The first Presbyterian mission was established on the Indian reservation in Polk County in 1881, and since then the church has played a major role in the lives of these Indians. Early missionaries served as teachers, ministers, doctors, nurses, and friends; their total impact is beyond measure. Dr. and Mrs. Caleb W. Chambers, whose dedication to their tasks was complete, served as missionaries among the Polk County Indians for thirty-eight years, beginning in 1899.

The third prominent influence was the work of J. C. Feagin of Livingston, Texas. Judge Feagin maintained a constant barrage of letters, reports, demands, and appeals on behalf of the area's Indian tribes to state and national officials at all levels of government. His efforts, which occupied nearly half a century before his death in 1927, successfully brought to the attention of the federal government the conditions and needs of the Alabamas and Coushattas; and his work was but the successful first phase of a campaign which would dramatically improve the lot of these Indians.

RESERVATION EXPANSION: In 1928 Clem Fain, Jr., of Livingston was appointed agent for the Polk County Indians. He continued the campaign to focus public attention on the Alabamas and Coushattas. Early in 1928 he accompanied Chief Charles Martin Thompson and Speaker Chief McConico Battise to Washington to appeal for assistance.

The campaign was successful: the federal government purchased an additional 3,071 acres adjoining the original reservation. The deed for this additional land was issued to the Alabama and Coushatta Indian Tribes, and the name "Alabama-Coushatta" has been used since 1928 as the official title of this enlarged reservation of 4,181.7 acres.

THE HOWARD N. MARTIN COLLECTION of Alabama-Coushatta myths and folktales was assembled during the decade of the 1930s. Because the foregoing discussion is intended to provide the historical context in which contemporary versions of these stories developed, rather than to delineate Alabama-Coushatta history as an end in itself, it seems appropriate to conclude these notes on historical highlights with the final major event before the tales were transcribed—enlargement of the Alabama-Coushatta reservation.

A documentary history of these two tribes, covering in detail the entire period from the first records to the present, is being prepared by the editor for future publication. That volume will highlight turning points in the history of the Alabamas and Coushattas. Many of the turning points have been discussed, albeit briefly, in the preceding notes on historical background for the tales; but it should be noted that in recent years there have been several significant changes which in the aggregate have had a major impact on Alabama-Coushatta life. These changes include: improvement of physical facilities—roads, fencing, and a variety of buildings for the use of reservation residents and their visitors; a self-help housing program; improved health and medical facilities; expanded educational opportunities; a wide-ranging program to attract tourists; renewed confidence among the Alabamas and Coushattas in their drive toward self-sufficiency.

COMMENTS ON THE ALABAMA-COUSHATTA NARRATIVES

The 46 prose narratives in this publication include a wide range of story themes, including the creation of the earth, strange adventures of remote ancestors, animal exploits and origins of animal characteristics, hero tales, and adventure stories involving magic, spirits, cannibals, monsters, transformation, and deception. These stories are not a complete compendium of Alabama-Coushatta folklore, but merely a representative selection of tales preserved into the 1930s.

Many of these stories belong to a period which is long past and cannot be repeated in our world. The majority fall into either of two classifications: myth or folktale.

Myths are considered to be essentially truthful accounts of the origins of the natural order and of culture; they explain the source of man and the world he inhabits. Narratives of this type deal with the transition from a mythological period to the modern age.[1] They describe characters and relate incidents which happened—so the Alabama-Coushatta storytellers say—during a formative time when the world, its inhabitants, and its social order had not assumed their present characteristics.

Folktales, on the other hand, usually focus on the adventures of animals or human characters—and one often finds animals with human characteristics and faculties interacting with humans as part of a larger "society." These stories are virtually timeless and placeless, and usually are told primarily for amusement.[2]

Three stories in a third classification—local legends—have been added to represent tales told by the Alabamas and Coushattas about their tribal history during comparatively recent times. Legends are accounts of extraordinary events believed actually to have occurred. They deal with historical characters, are definitely localized, and relate directly to tribes of today.[3] Unlike myths and folktales, local legends are specific to a tribe (or to interrelated tribes, such as the Alabamas and Coushattas); they are not represented in the verbal traditions of other tribes.

Alabama-Coushatta informants of the 1930s invariably pointed out that the stories of a misty past were believed by the "old people" but no longer were accepted as true by tribal members. Why were these stories told? What were the objectives of the ancient storytellers?

There is no evidence which permits us to answer these questions directly. Scholarly analysis, however, provides clear indications that oral traditions, transmitting folklore from one generation to another, served definite purposes. Stith Thompson has written that North American Indian tales generally served five interrelated functions: (1) to satisfy yearnings for information about the past; (2) to furnish religious edification; (3) to exhort listeners to perform heroic deeds; (4) to provide amusement; and (5) to afford release from the overpowering monotony of day-to-day life.[4] While all of these purposes may have been served in bygone years, Alabama-Coushatta informants during the 1930s emphasized that the tales no longer were told for any reason other than amusement.

Certain characteristic literary features may be noted in Alabama-Coushatta narratives. These are discussed below.

DIFFUSION: North American Indians, in the days before United States expansion engendered a policy of confinement to reservations, had extensive intertribal contacts. The existence of well-known and high-traffic trade routes, trade jargon, political alliances (often involving several tribes), nomadic or quasi-nomadic migration, and intertribal wars suggests a multiplicity of contacts and associations among Indian tribes over an extended period.[5]

One consequence of such frequent and sustained contacts is the widespread diffusion of story elements—not only motifs, but also specific events. Most tales known to one tribe are likely to be known, albeit often in variant forms, to tribes in adjacent territories. Indeed, tales were exchanged not only among tribes within culture areas, but sometimes between culture areas to the extent that a given tale may be found among tribes spanning the continent.[6]

The principal elements of Alabama and Coushatta narratives, with the exception of those in the category of local legends, appear to be common to nearly all North American tribes. Although occasional incidents are unique to Alabama-Coushatta folklore and must have originated indigenously, it is improbable that any substantial part of the stories in this collection arose independently among the Alabamas and Coushattas.

EXPLANATION: The use of explanatory incidents is a prominent feature of Indian myths and folktales. A limited number of such stories have explanation as their primary objective; but for most, the explanatory element is an appendage added for reasons not directly concerned with the plot.[7]

This generalized statement applies to the stories in this collection. Explanations appear frequently, usually as "postscripts." One can readily determine when explanation is not the main objective of the tale: either the explanation is extraneous or a logically more appropriate conclusion suggests itself.

Why, then, the prevalence of explanatory addenda to many of these tales? Comments by five of the Alabama-Coushatta informants parallel the findings of folklore researchers who have pointed out that the explanation often serves as the "proof" of the story.[8] To provide verification for his tale, an Indian storyteller might add an incident about an animal or bird so the story would carry conviction. For example, after recounting "The Bungling Host," an Alabama-Coushatta informant said, "If you do not believe what I told you about Rabbit injuring himself while trying to imitate Bear, just look at Buzzard and you will see his nostrils that were enlarged by blowgun arrows."

MAGIC: Franz Boas wrote that belief in magic power is a fundamental concept among all Indian tribes. The concept is reciprocal, according to Boas: magic power may influence the lives of men—but may, in turn, be influenced by human activity.[9]

Ancestors of today's Alabamas and Coushattas shared the belief in magical powers superior to man's natural capabilities, and this belief is reflected throughout this collection of tales in incidents in which men act to gain and retain the good will of the animals, beings, spirits, or inanimate objects that have magic powers.

Magic appears in these stories as an integral component of the natural order; it is part of everyday life. The original audiences for these tales accepted the reality, or at least the possibility, of magical occurrences and objects. By contrast, children today must willfully suspend belief in the inviolability of natural laws when viewing cartoons which show acts and events impossible in the "real" world.

The prevalence of magic in Alabama-Coushatta folklore has altered perceptibly over time. In tales clearly of earlier origin, the world is infused with magic: magical powers are used routinely, as in hunting preparations and hunting paraphernalia, and also appear in heightened form when associated with extraordinary events, such as overcoming superhuman creatures. In stories of more recent origin, however, the use of magical elements becomes more restricted: magical powers are ascribed only to special or extraordinary individuals.

NUMBER OF REPETITIONS AND OCCURRENCES: In European folklore, the number three is used widely in relation to daily happenings. Among a majority of North American Indian tribes, the corresponding number is four: repetitious elements or events usually occur four times in myths and folktales.[10]

This trait is not found so extensively in Alabama-Coushatta narratives. In the stories in this collection, the number three is used more frequently than the number four. One may question whether this characteristic is attributable to alteration in the tales, as a function of contact with a society of European origin, during the two centuries preceding their recording; but such a question appears to be beyond resolution.

The use of "three" in Alabama-Coushatta tales is not restricted to certain types of stories, but appears throughout the collection. For example, Turtle agreed to race Fox three days after their meeting, on a course that extended over three hills, and he asked three friends to help him deceive Fox. Three horses were required to carry venison provided by the orphan in "The Dirty Boy." The hero had to cut off a cannibal's head the third time, because the head reunited with the cannibal's body after it had been severed twice. The mythical Crawfish was the third creature that tried to swim to the bottom of the primeval ocean to obtain dirt that would make land appear.

NARRATIVE SECTIONS: Stories in this collection are grouped in eleven major sections (Parts I-XI) which are intended to reflect the dominant spirit and themes of the narratives. This arrangement is a matter of convenience, and should not be regarded as a hard-and-fast typology: while some tales clearly belong in the categories to which they have been assigned, others contain a mixture of elements which makes their assignment to one of the sections more ambiguous. The reader, then, may disagree with particular judgments made in grouping these tales; it is hoped merely that the general arrangement according to commonality of content will prove helpful.

PART I. MYTHOLOGICAL INCIDENTS: The stories in this group are either cosmogonic or cosmologic: they relate to the creation of the universe and the development of the universe as an orderly system, focusing on changes which had to occur before the earth became habitable for men. To show how the present order (natural phenomena and cultural characteristics) arose in the world, the storytellers' techniques usually involved selecting features of the contemporary world, describing the features as they were alleged to have existed during the primeval period, and then explaining changes in these features as consequences of events during the period of transition from primeval to contemporary order.

Myths explaining the origin of dry land were widely disseminated among North American Indians, and nearly every tribe was acquainted with at least one such myth. Widespread diffusion of myths gave rise to numerous variants.[11]

One of the most popular motifs regarding the appearance of land involved earth-divers: various animals attempted to dive to the bottom of a great ocean to obtain a small quantity of sand or other materials to make the earth appear. In the Alabama-Coushatta earth-diver story, Crawfish was the successful diver after Beaver and Frog failed. Instead of bringing up a small quantity of earth in his claws, as in versions related by other tribes, Crawfish built a mud chimney that eventually reached the surface of the water.

The Alabama-Coushattas related two versions of this story. The incidents described are identical, with one exception. In the version selected for this publication, three creatures—Beaver, Frog, and Crawfish—attempted to dive to the bottom of the great ocean to make land appear. In the alternate version, Crawfish was the only earth-diver; his first two dives ended in failure, but on the third dive, he reached the bottom of the primeval sea.

The earth created as a result of the earth-diver's efforts was conceived to be a flat plane overarched by a solid vault or sky resembling a great bowl inverted over the earth. The ancient world was conceived to be a hollow chamber between a solid dome and a horizontal earth. The sun, moon, and stars traveled their appointed paths along the face of this dome.

At regular intervals, according to Alabama-Coushatta folklore, this domed vault rose and fell upon the edge of the earth so that the space at the juncture was opening and closing constantly—like a pair of scissors. By carefully gauging his opportunity, a person could pass under the edge of the dome and enter a spirit-land very much like the earth, with vegetation and inhabitants.

The story of a great deluge is known throughout the world. Although this story resembles in certain details the experiences of Noah recorded in the Book of Genesis, a majority of North American Indian tribes are known to have had similar myths of purely native origin.[12]

The stories which appear in Part I of this collection are primarily mythological in nature, but mythological motifs also occur in other narratives selected for this publication. A complete list of the mythological motifs in all of these stories appears in the appendix, where motifs are numbered AO-A2899.

PART II. ORIGINS OF ANIMAL AND BIRD CHARACTERISTICS: Animals (including birds) are featured prominently in the folklore of the Alabamas and Coushattas; often they are the principal actors. In mythological tales, animals sometimes appear as cosmic creative agencies: Crawfish, for example, built a mud chimney from the bottom of the primeval ocean to make land appear. Most of the stories in this collection, however, are centered around animal exploits and how animals acquired their distinguishing characteristics.

Stories in Part II reflect Alabama-Coushatta observations of the wild creatures in the tribal environment. At the beginning of historical records pertaining to these two tribes, they were living in the woodlands of the southeastern United States, primarily in the present state of Alabama. In their westward migration, the Alabamas and Coushattas settled temporarily in Louisiana before moving to the Big Thicket of East Texas, and in both of these regions they lived in areas not unlike their homeland along the Alabama River.

Wildlife was essentially the same in all areas inhabited by the Alabamas and Coushattas, and storytellers in these two tribes had ample opportunity for observations on which to base narratives explaining color, size, shape, and other characteristics of wild creatures.

The animals in these narratives had chiefs, councils, and square-grounds, reflecting Alabama-Coushatta social organization. Many lived in cabins like those typically built by these tribes. Often animals in these tales are part of a single social system in which they are either co-equal with or subordinate to people; at many other points, the animals are found mingling with people and speaking their language. Such anthropomorphism is a prominent feature of these stories.

Each animal, moreover, had his appointed station and duty—although both may vary from one tale to another. The common time-frame for the majority of these tales lies in that period which the Alabamas and Coushattas conceived to precede the establishment of the present natural and social order.

Animals in Alabama-Coushatta folklore often personify certain traits and characteristics. Rabbit is dominant in this respect: he is consistently the trickster and mischief maker. A discussion of his activities and exploits is included in the notes for Part IV.

Turtle was regarded as the type of plodding slowness, while the rabbit, fox, and deer represented speed. In his comments on races between the two types, James Mooney asked: "What more natural than that the storyteller should set one to race against the other, with the victory in favor of the patient striver against the self-confident boaster?"[13]

Although the motif of a race between these two types is common to many tribes, the Alabama-Coushatta version is unique in two respects. First, Turtle's opponent in this race is Fox, while in the lore of other tribes from the same region, Turtle races Rabbit. Second, the race between Turtle and his opponent is usually an independent tale, but in the Alabama-Coushatta variant this race is only part of a longer story which explains the patchwork appearance of Turtle's shell.

In verbal traditions, it is common for story elements to be shifted among tales, allowing the creation of endless varieties. This phenomenon is apparent in Alabama-Coushatta stories, most notably in tales involving the origins of animal characteristics: while some of the tales are designed to explain such origins, many others use a brief observation of an animal's distinguishing feature as "proof" of the veracity of the logically unrelated story content.

PART III. AFTERWORLD TRIP: In North American Indian narratives, there usually is no manifest distinction between events and conditions of this world and the afterworld. After death, individuals supposedly travel to a spirit-land and remain there, living as they had on earth.[14]

References to a dual afterworld with reward and punishment are very rare among American Indians.[15] The Alabamas and Coushattas recognized only an upper world. The mythological origin of these two tribes from clay and their emergence from a cave provide the only evidence that at some time in the distant past ancient Alabamas and Coushattas might have believed in a lower world; and the intent of the sole story in which this motif occurs—to explain the minor differences between Alabamas and Coushattas, and to explain their small numbers—indicates that even in this instance one would be hard-pressed to argue cogently the existence of a dual-afterworld concept.

In "A Journey to the Sky," three men made the trip to the afterworld along the route which souls of the deceased are required to travel. This story provides a clear-cut indication of Alabama-Coushatta conceptions of the afterworld. To these two tribes, life after death meant a continuation of present conditions insofar as wants and means of satisfaction were concerned. It was believed that in the afterworld each person would need what he had needed or found useful on earth, and a variety of personal items was buried with the body of the deceased.

On the journey to the afterworld, the soul of each deceased had to encounter several dangerous obstacles. An immense body of water and a place filled with snakes were among the traveler's hazardous problems. A great eagle attacked anyone moving along the path to the afterworld, and a large knife was buried with each deceased to be used in fighting this fierce bird. The final obstacle was crossing under the domed sky as it rose and fell at the edge of the earth. (See notes relating to narratives in Part I.)

The sole tale in Part III is intriguing because it presents the saga of three lifelong friends who determined to make the journey—and because two of them returned to the village to recount what they had experienced. This story shares with those in the mythological category the feature that explanation of a type—exposition of the nature of the afterworld—is central rather than peripheral to the plot. It shares with the folktale category the element of "proof" at the end of the story: the two survivors return to their village to proclaim what they had experienced and to distribute seeds which, when cultivated, produced plants the villagers had not seen previously.

In strict terms, then, this narrative is a hybrid: it illuminates an aspect of the world order which appears to have been central, and it also provides a "proof" which is not a necessary ingredient of the plot.

PART IV. TRICKSTER CYCLE: Among the Alabamas and Coushattas the most popular type of story involved a trickster, and this popularity is evident today in conversations with residents on the Alabama-

Coushatta reservation. The trickster in the stories of these two tribes is Rabbit, who is the principal hero and the author of mischief.

The adventures of the trickster are inconsistent. Part are the result of his stupidity, but most show him overcoming his enemies through cleverness.[16]

The various roles of Rabbit are indicated below, and for illustrative purposes, a story from Part IV is listed after each role: beneficent hero ("Rabbit Plays Pranks on Big Man-Eater"); amorous adventurer ("Why Rabbit Has Big Eyes and Long Ears"); clever deceiver ("The Buffalo Tug-of-War"); cheater ("Rabbit Outwits a Farmer"); numbskull or dupe ("The Bungling Host"); swindler ("The Tasks of Rabbit"); glutton ("Rabbit and the Turkeys").

PART V. ADVENTURES WITH CANNIBALS: The cannibals in these stories were ogres in human form. In appearance they resembled members of any other tribe living near them. Their cannibalistic practices were reserved for unwary travelers or members of enemy tribes whom they captured.

Alabama-Coushatta informants did not know how these cannibal stories originated. Incidents in both stories in Part V involve demonstrations of magic power, which might suggest that the stories began long ago near the transition from a primeval period to the modern age.

Information available at a later period also might have been used by the storytellers in organizing these cannibal stories. Atakapans and other tribes along the Louisiana and Texas coasts were genuine practitioners of cannibalism,[17] and news of their activities could have provided the basic material for the cannibal incidents in these stories.

The second story in Part V features the "Magic Flight" motif which Franz Boas cited as an example of worldwide dissemination. He pointed out that this story was introduced into North America in two currents: an ancient one from Siberia by way of the Bering Strait, and a more recent one from Spain via South America and then extending northward. This narrative is organized around two elements: (1) flight from an ogre; and (2) objects thrown down to form obstacles—in the Alabama-Coushatta variant, first ripe huckleberries which became huckleberry bushes, then blackberries which instantly formed a blackberry thicket to delay the pursuer, next three pieces of cane to produce a dense canebrake, and finally mud, causing the trail behind the intended victim to become boggy.[18]

PART VI. GHOSTS, WITCHES, AND OTHER SUPERNATURAL

BEINGS: John R. Swanton wrote that the southern Indians (including Alabamas and Coushattas) believed that something supernatural inhered in every created thing—every animal, plant, stone, stick, body of water, geographical feature, and even in objects man himself had made.[19]

Environment was a major factor in the development of these beliefs. Dense forests—in the Big Thicket and in other similar areas—surrounding the homes of the Alabamas and Coushattas were regarded as the habitat of mysterious beings to whom were attributed injuries to hunters, unusual sounds, and natural phenomena. The Alabamas and Coushattas considered themselves to be surrounded at all times by supernatural beings, who would make themselves visible to travelers in the dense forests or would indicate their presence by weird sounds.

One of the fundamental characteristic beliefs held generally by Indians was the utter helplessness of man against his environment when unaided by the magic power of some favoring being. Most of the beings by which they believed themselves surrounded were purely imaginary.[20]

Included among the supernatural beings are spirits, good and bad. Paul Radin stated that North American Indians have peopled their universe with spirits as real as man but more powerful than man. They are conceived as visible, audible, felt emotionally, or manifesting their existence by some sign or result. Also, spirits possess the power of bestowing upon man all things of social or economic value to him. Means of bringing spirits into relation with man include fasting, mental concentration, self-castigation and torture, offerings and sacrifices, prayers and incantations, charms and fetishes.[21]

J. W. Powell described ghosts as magical beings who perform their wonders by necromancy, so magic can be used to influence and coerce ghosts to subserve human purposes. Medicine men have the power to control ghosts for any or every purpose.[22]

Witchcraft is the practice of sorcery for evil purposes.[23] Medicine men frequently attributed sickness to the activities of witches, and witchcraft was given as the reason for killing certain persons, usually old women. John R. Swanton pointed out, however, that a witch was killed not because he or she possessed the powers of a wizard, but rather because it was believed the witch had killed or seriously injured someone else.[24]

PART VII. ANIMAL AND BIRD HUSBANDS: One motif found throughout this collection is the ascription of human roles to animals. Earlier it was noted that these tales often feature animals with human characteristics and faculties interacting with humans as part of a larger society. Such is the extent to which this motif is used that it is not always clear whether the storyteller is referring to human or to animal actors.

The two stories in Part VII represent a particular facet of this motif: marriage between humans and animals. Such marriages are not at all uncommon in North American Indian folktales. The two narratives in this collection involve a buffalo and an owl as animal husbands for human wives.

The first of these two stories involves the "Flight to the Tree" motif, which is widely diffused in North America. It also offers excellent examples of the role of magic, which was discussed in the general comments on Alabama-Coushatta narratives.

PART VIII. ENCOUNTERS WITH MONSTERS: The monsters presented in this group of narratives are not exaggerated human figures, but extraordinarily large animals—lizard, panther, and deer. Great beasts also appear in other sections of this collection—for example, the elephant or Big Man-Eater in Part IV and the horned snake in Parts III and VII.

Stories in this section bear the mark of more recent origin than do those presented at earlier points in the collection. The tales involving the panther and the deer clearly indicate the tendency to restrict magic to particularly extraordinary creatures or people in unusual situations, and the story of the monster lizard is devoid of magic.

The source material for such stories is a matter for speculation, but it is not unreasonable to suppose that the occasional discovery of large bones in fossil form gave rise to imaginative creation of monster creatures.

Inordinately large creatures furnished the occasion for attribution of special abilities; one can easily imagine that the discovery of evidence that creatures far larger than anything within the experience of persons living at the time was *prima facie* evidence that, because these creatures were *different,* they must have had unique faculties. The helpful talking panther is one example.

By the same token, the incorporation of large beasts into Alabama-Coushatta tales (as into tales of other tribes) provided the occasion for using these creatures as storytelling mechanisms to overcome otherwise insurmountable obstacles. With imagination guiding reality to the fulfillment of wishes, one finds such instances as Horned Snake—big enough to carry three men—unwittingly providing transportation across a large body of water.

Large beasts, especially those which are usually regarded as fearsome, also offer the storyteller the opportunity to give fear material form. The two tales which present the monster lizard as hunter—and especially the story in which the monster lizard trails his human opponents singly, killing all but the last—are excellent examples of such embodiment of fear in animal form.

PART IX. HERO STORIES: A substantial number of North American Indian tales relate to the exploits of heroes who overcome seemingly invincible adversaries.[25] Orrin E. Klapp has identified ten common roles of heroes: feat, contest, test, quest, clever hero, unpromising hero, defender or deliverer, benefactor, culture hero, and martyr.[26]

The principal hero roles represented in the Alabama-Coushatta narratives are indicated below with references to corresponding stories in the collection.

1. TEST: The hero is subjected to a series of tests, or he undertakes to overcome monsters or other adversaries of his own volition.[27] ("A Trip to the Bead-Spitter")

2. QUEST: This role involves a prolonged endeavor toward a goal and includes a series of feats and tests before final attainment.[28] ("A Journey to the Sky")

3. CLEVER HERO: This popular symbol teaches that the weak can defeat the great and points out that ruse is often more effective than force.[29] ("The Escape from an Eagle," "The Buffalo Tug-of-War," "Rabbit Outwits a Farmer," "Rabbit Plays Pranks on Big Man-Eater," and other stories about the exploits of the rabbit)

4. UNPROMISING HERO: This is the role of the "dark horse," the poor, unfortunate person who achieves success. The unpromising person is derided or persecuted by rivals before his unexpected triumph.[30] ("The Dirty Boy")

5. DEFENDER OR DELIVERER: This role relates to the hero who comes to rescue a person or a group from danger.[31] ("The Man with Horns," "The Pigeon Hawk's Gift")

PART X. HISTORICAL SKETCHES: Local legends have been defined elsewhere in these comments as stories about tribal history during comparatively recent times. The three stories in Part X are localized and are found only in narratives of the Alabamas and Coushattas.

The Tombigbee River in western Alabama formed a substantial part of the boundary between the very large Choctaw Indian tribe and the tribes of the Creek Confederacy, including the Alabamas and Coushattas. In the eighteenth century the Choctaws were almost constantly at war with the Alabamas and Coushattas.

The second story in this group recounts the westward migration of the Alabamas, as told by members of this tribe. This legend was recorded originally by John R. Swanton,[32] and it is included in this group with only minor changes suggested by tribal informants in the 1930s.

Colita lived in the Lower Coushatta Village in a great bend of the Trinity River—the "shirt-tail bend," as the steamboat sailors named it— in present San Jacinto County. He was one of the best-known Indian leaders in East Texas and succeeded Long King as principal chief of the Coushatta Tribe a few years after the Republic of Texas gained independence from Mexico.

PART XI. MISCELLANEOUS TALES: Parts I through X include the principal classes of Alabama-Coushatta narratives. The selection of the label, "Miscellaneous," for the Part XI stories is not intended to reflect pejoratively on these four tales: each of the four is important, but none seems to fit any of the major classes in Parts I-X.

The Alabama-Coushatta narratives reflect belief in a variety of supernatural beings, including pygmies or "little people." These small beings frighten men and do them mischief, but rarely if ever cause lasting damage. Additional comments relating to pygmies may be found in the glossary.

Indians generally believed in transformation, in which a person, animal, or object may be magically changed into another person, animal, or object. In the second story of Part XI, a man ate fish in violation of a taboo and, as a result, was transformed into a "tie-snake."

"The Escape from an Eagle" is a variant of a story widely diffused in the western United States. This story describes the actions of a clever hero who escapes from a great eagle and then performs an unusual feat by riding another eagle from the top of a mountain to the ground.

The concluding story in Part XI probably is based on material from the Bible: the conceptualization of Aba Mikko as the supreme deity and the introduction of a son of the deity who comes to earth to restore peace among Aba Mikko's children not only parallel Biblical accounts, but also present motifs not found elsewhere in Alabama-Coushatta tales. The "blind dupe" motif, while it does not conform to accounts of the crucifixion directly, incorporates elements consistent with other gospel accounts. This story is an excellent example of the absorption of key elements from one culture into the oral tradition of another.

MOTIFS IN ALABAMA-COUSHATTA NARRATIVES: The motifs in the stories of this collection are listed by story in the appendix. This arrangement of motifs was prepared to expedite the work of those who wish to use these narratives in comparative studies or in other types of analyses.

NOTES

[1] Franz Boas, "Mythology and Folk-Tales of the North American Indians," *Journal of American Folklore*, 27 (1914), 404-410; Stith Thompson, *The Folktale*, (New York: The Dryden Press, 1946), p. 9; William Bascom, "The Forms of Folklore: Prose Narratives," *Journal of American Folklore*, 78, No. 307 (1965), 4.

[2] Bascom, "The Forms of Folklore," 4.

[3] Thompson, *The Folktale*, pp. 8-9; Bascom, "The Forms of Folklore," 4-5.

[4] Thompson, *The Folktale*, p. 3.

[5] James Mooney, "Myths of the Cherokee," *Nineteenth Annual Report of the Bureau of American Ethnology*, (Washington, D.C.: Government Printing Office, 1900), pp. 234-235.

[6] T. T. Waterman, "The Explanatory Element in the Folk-Tales of the North American Indians," *Journal of American Folk-Lore*, 27, No. 103 (1914), 34; Thompson, *The Folktale*, pp. 301-302.

[7] Waterman, "The Explanatory Element," 10, 20-21, 27, 33, 37-38, 40-41.

[8] Waterman, "The Explanatory Element," 39; Robert H. Lowie, "The Test-Theme in North American Mythology," *Journal of American Folklore*, 21, Nos. 81-82 (1908), 123-124.

[9] Franz Boas, "Religion," in *Handbook of American Indians North of Mexico*, Part 2, Frederick Webb Hodge, ed. (Washington, D.C.: Government Printing Office, 1912), pp. 365-371.

[10] Stith Thompson, *Tales of the North American Indians*, (Cambridge: Harvard University Press, 1929), pp. 350-351.

[11] Albert S. Gatschet, "Some Mythic Stories of the Yuchi Indians," *American Anthropologist*, 6, Old Series (1893), 279.

Introduction

[12]Thompson, *The Folktale*, p. 313.

[13]Mooney, "Myths of the Cherokee," p. 234.

[14]Thompson, *The Folktale*, p. 345; Paul Radin, "Religion of the North American Indians," *Journal of American Folk-Lore*, 27, No. 106 (1914), 370-371.

[15]Thompson, *The Folktale*, 351; T.N. Campbell, "The Choctaw Afterworld," *Journal of American Folklore*, 72, No. 284, (1959), 153.

[16]Thompson, *The Folktale*, p. 319.

[17]John R. Swanton, "Aboriginal Culture of the Southeast," *Forty-Second Annual Report of the Bureau of American Ethnology*, (Washington, D.C.: Government Printing Office, 1928), pp. 705, 712-713.

[18]Boas, "Mythology and Folk-Tales," 381, 386.

[19]John R. Swanton, "Religious Beliefs and Medical Practices of the Creek Indians," *Forty-Second Annual Report of the Bureau of American Ethnology*, (Washington, D.C.: Government Printing Office, 1928), p. 489.

[20]Hodge, *Handbook of American Indians*, p. 967.

[21]Radin, "Religion of the North American Indians," 352-353, 357, 366-369.

[22]J. W. Powell, "The Lessons of Folklore," *American Anthropologist*, 2, New Series (1900), 13-14.

[23]J. W. Powell, *Outlines of the Philosophy of the North American Indians*, (New York: Douglas Taylor, Printer, 1877), p. 14.

[24]John R. Swanton, "Social Organization and Social Usages of the Indians of the Creek Confederacy," *Forty-Second Annual Report of the Bureau of American Ethnology*, (Washington, D.C.: Government Printing Office, 1928), pp. 345-346.

[25]Thompson, *The Folktale*, p. 329.

[26]Orrin E. Klapp, "The Folk Hero," *Journal of American Folklore*, 62, No. 243 (1949), 19.

[27]Ibid.

[28]Ibid.

[29]Ibid., 20.

[30]Ibid.

[31]Ibid., 21.

[32]John R. Swanton, *Myths and Tales of the Southeastern Indians*, Bureau of American Ethnology, Bulletin 88, (Washington, D.C.: Government Printing Office, 1929), pp. 118-121.

Notes xxxvii

Part I

Mythological Incidents

CREATION OF THE EARTH

ONCE, long ago, before the time of the oldest people, water covered everything. The only living creatures above the water were some small animals and birds who occupied a log raft drifting about on the great ocean. Nothing else could be seen above the surface of the water.

Each day the occupants on the large raft looked in all directions, but all they saw was water and the sky. The birds would fly out from the raft hoping to find land, but always there was just water. Soon the occupants of the raft grew restless and began talking about how to find land. They chose Horned Owl to be their council chief.

During their discussion one day, Horned Owl said, "Land is somewhere beneath the water. We must make it appear or we will starve. Who will look for land?"

Beaver spoke first and said, "I am a good swimmer. I will try."

Then Beaver dived into the water and swam toward the bottom. He was a strong swimmer, and at first he moved rapidly through the water. The water was very deep, however, and after he had been swimming for a long time and still did not reach the bottom, he began to tire. Eventually he had to give up the search for land and return to the raft.

Horned Owl called for another volunteer. This time Frog said he would look for land. He jumped into the water and started swimming for the bottom, but Garfish chased him and forced Frog to return to the raft.

Again Horned Owl spoke with the raft creatures of the need to make land appear. At the end of his talk, Horned Owl asked Crawfish to look for land.

"Yes, I am ready," answered Crawfish. "I will go now."

Then Crawfish jumped into the water and swam toward the bottom. Garfish did not think he looked good to eat and did not chase him. Crawfish was also a better swimmer than Beaver and did not tire so easily, and so he came to the bottom of the great ocean.

Now, Crawfish has a wide tail which he can use as a scoop. When he reached the bottom of the water, he used his tail to scoop mud into a great chimney. He worked rapidly, building it higher and higher, until the top of the mud chimney stuck up above the water, where it began to spread and form a mass of soft earth.

The birds and animals on the raft looked at the new earth and agreed that Crawfish had done a good job, but they thought the earth was too smooth. So Horned Owl sent Buzzard out to shape the earth's surface.

Buzzard was a huge bird with long, powerful wings. He flew along just above the soft earth, flapping his wings. When he swung his wings down, he made valleys in the earth. When he swept his wings up, he formed the hills and mountains. During the time that Buzzard glided along without flapping his wings, he made level country and plains.

After the earth had hardened, the animals and birds left their raft and made homes in the new land, each according to his needs.

ORIGIN OF THE ALABAMA AND COUSHATTA TRIBES

THE Alabamas and Coushattas were made from clay in a big cave under the earth. They lived in this cave a long time before some of them decided to go to the surface of the earth. After they started upward, they camped three times on the way. Finally, they reached the mouth of the cave.

Here they saw that a large tree stood in the cave entrance. The Alabamas and Coushattas went out of the cave on opposite sides of a root of this big tree. This is why these two tribes differ somewhat in speech, though they always have lived near each other.

At first these people stayed outside only during the night, returning to the cave when day came. One night when they left the cave to play, they heard an owl hooting. Most of the people became so scared that they ran back into the cave and never returned to the surface of the earth. This is why the Alabamas and Coushattas are so few. Had the owl not hooted, all the people would have remained on the surface of the earth, and the Alabamas and Coushattas would be more numerous.

ABA MIKKO ARRANGES THE MONTHS AND SEASONS

WHEN Aba Mikko made the months of the year, he gave each bird and animal the month of its choice. As soon as Aba Mikko molded a month and put it down to ripen, the bird or animal who desired that month took it and ran off with it.

Likewise, Aba Mikko divided other things among the earth creatures. He gave all the grass on earth to Horse and told Bear and Squirrel they could have all the acorns. Birds like to eat insects, so Aba Mikko gave all the insects to birds.

Then each bird and animal agreed to perform some sort of service. Horse said, "I will carry loads for people." Hummingbird said, "I will kiss the flowers." In like manner, each of the other creatures agreed to do something useful in gratitude for Aba Mikko's gifts.

Finally, the seasons—winter, spring, summer, and fall—were made at the same time. Winter said, "Man is going to roast his leg around me," meaning that people would stay near fires during the winter season. Since little work can be done during the summer, the hot season of the year is short.

At first the sun was very hot and burned all the plants on the earth. When the people asked Aba Mikko to help with this problem, he made the sun and moon exchange places. Thus, the original sun became the moon, while the original moon became the sun we see in the sky today.

Although the new sun was not so warm as the original sun, it was still too hot for people who lived far to the east and for others who lived in the west. Because the earth is flat, the sun is near the earth in the morning, very high above the earth at mid-day, and again close to the earth when it goes down.

The people living at the eastern and western edges of the flat earth did not have hair on their heads, so they were burned terribly while the sun was near the earth each day. Therefore, each morning the people in the east threw rocks at the sun, making it rise very fast. When the sun got so high the people could not hit it, the sun traveled slowly. When the sun started down in the west, however, the people in the west threw rocks at it, forcing the sun to set quickly.

The sun still follows this pattern in its daily journey through the sky.

THE ORIGIN OF CORN AND TOBACCO

LONG AGO six brothers lived in a large village of the Alabama tribe. These young men developed unusual skill in the use of bows and arrows. In time, the brothers gained reputations as the best hunters in their village.

One day the youngest brother left the village on a long hunting trip. On the first night, he camped at a place near which two strange men already had built a fire.

The next morning the two strangers called to the young hunter, "Come and eat with us."

The youth accepted this invitation and, after the three had finished the meal, he volunteered to take care of the camp while his hosts went hunting. When the two men walked away from the camp, the young man snapped his fingers against a clay pot which started growing larger. Into this pot he put food and water, and kept a fire beneath it until it boiled.

Although the young hunter wanted to help his new friends, they saddened when they returned near the end of the day and saw the dinner he had prepared. One of them said, "Everything is spoiled for us. We are spirits and cannot eat boiled food. Now we must leave you."

Before leaving, though, the spirit men went hunting with the young man. They found the trail of a bear, and the three hunters set out to tree the bear.

For three days they followed the bear, and on the fourth day the young hunter saw something in the trail that turned his attention from the bear hunt. He found two red kernels which the strangers said were corn.

Farther down the trail he found two more kernels of corn, which he picked up and carried with him. Still farther on, the young hunter again found several kernels in the path, and again he picked them up. Presently the trail of corn kernels ended, and in front of them the hunters saw a large field of ripe corn.

Then the two strangers told their young friend how to grow corn. They also taught him how to build corn cribs to store the crop at harvest.

Next, they gave him some tobacco seed and told him to plant it and, later, to dry it and smoke the leaves of the tobacco plants.

While the young hunter thought about his friends' gifts and instructions, the two spirit men disappeared. They had completed their mission to carry corn and tobacco to people on earth.

HOW THE SUN CAME TO THE SKY

IN a place where the Alabamas used to have a village, an old woman caught the sun and put it in a clay pot. Rabbit wanted the sun, but at first he did not know how to steal it from the old woman.

Now Rabbit was well-known for his ability as a dancer, so he finally decided to steal the sun by trickery. Accordingly, Rabbit invited all the people to come to the house of the sun-keeper, and then he said to the assembled crowd, "Sing for me so I can dance."

"We don't know how to sing for you," they answered.

"Sing 'Rabbit, Rabbit, Rabbit,' " he said.

So they sang "Rabbit, Rabbit, Rabbit," and he danced.

While Rabbit danced, he said, "Move the sun toward me." And the unsuspecting people moved it toward him.

Again Rabbit said, "Move the sun toward me. I am dancing like a crazy person."

When the people moved the sun closer to Rabbit, he suddenly picked it up and ran into the forest. The people chased Rabbit but could not catch him. As Rabbit ran along, the earthen pot struck some bushes, but it did not break. Finally, Rabbit accidentally ran into an oak tree, and this time the pot broke into many pieces.

Soon all the creatures gathered around the sun, which Rabbit left near the oak tree. They held a council and decided to set the sun up in the sky.

Wren tried to move the sun, but rose only a short distance above the earth before falling back again. He said, "If another would help me, I could carry it up."

At first none of the other birds wanted to help Wren. They were afraid to fly so high. Finally, Buzzard said he would help. Then Wren and Buzzard caught hold of the sun and flew up with it. After fastening the sun in the sky, Buzzard and Wren returned to the earth.

The people agreed that these two birds should be rewarded, so they said to Buzzard, "You shall eat animals that have died." Then they said to Wren, "You shall wash in cold water every morning so you will never be sick."

HOW WATER WAS LOST AND RECOVERED

THE Alabamas and Coushattas have a game which is played with four square pieces of deer hide placed upon a big bear-skin laid down hair side up.

After the players form two sides, one player takes a small pebble and moves it about in his hands, pretending to put it under the pieces of deer hide. Finally he deposits it under one piece of hide when he thinks his placement of the stone will escape observation.

An opponent then guesses which skin it has been placed under and, if he is successful, his party takes the pebble. If he fails, he guesses a second time, after the rock has been hidden again. If he fails three times, another of his party tries his skill.

One time Water-Keeper, who had been appointed guardian of all the water in the world, began betting his personal possessions on this guessing game. Soon he had lost everything he had, and then he started betting other things. Finally, he wagered all the water of the world and lost that, whereupon all the rivers, lakes, and other reservoirs of water dried up. All the inhabitants of the earth were slowly dying of thirst, but no one knew how to get water.

Soon Water-Keeper felt sorry and asked Aba Mikko to forgive him. Then Aba Mikko directed Woodpecker to a cane as big as a tree. The bird lighted on this big cane and began pecking. But before he had made much of a hole, he heard a noise inside that frightened him, and he flew away. Later Woodpecker returned to the big cane and pecked a hole all the way through. Water started running out so fast that all the rivers, creeks, and lakes were filled in three days. Then all the creatures drank and were happy again.

HOW FIRE CAME TO THE ALABAMAS AND COUSHATTAS

THERE was a time, far back, when bears owned Fire. These animals guarded Fire very closely and even carried it about with them. They allowed no creature except a member of the bear clan to use Fire or even to approach it.

One day the bears put Fire on the ground and went away to eat acorns. Now, Fire needed much attention. Since the bears did not come back that day, Fire grew weaker and weaker, and finally began calling for help. But the bears had traveled so far into the woods that they couldn't hear Fire's cries.

Some Alabamas and Coushattas heard him, though, and hurried to his aid. They got a stick from the north and laid it on Fire. In the west they found another stick and fed it to Fire. The people found the third stick in the south. Then they went to the east for another stick. When the people put down all of the sticks, Fire blazed up.

After the bears finished their meal of acorns, they returned to claim Fire. However, Fire said, "I don't know the bears any longer."

This is how Fire left the bears and went to live with the Alabamas and Coushattas.

WHY SICKNESS STILL EXISTS ON THE EARTH

LONG AGO, before the white man came to the country of the Alabamas and Coushattas, sickness was causing much trouble and grief everywhere. The people met in council and decided to get rid of sickness. Consequently, they collected all the sickness of the world and shut it up in a clay pot.

The chief then asked, "Who will take the pot into the sky and leave it?"

For days the chief went among the birds repeating this question, but none of the winged creatures wanted to make the trip. Finally, Snipe said he would try it.

"I will take sickness so far into the sky that it can never return to earth," boasted the confident bird.

To prove his ability, Snipe flew into the sky and quickly disappeared. When Snipe returned to earth, the chief tied the clay pot containing sickness to Snipe's legs. Then the bird started his upward flight. Up and up he flew until he could no longer be seen by the people, who were rejoicing that sickness would never again cause unhappiness in the world.

Shortly afterward the people saw Snipe returning to earth. To their surprise and disappointment, Snipe was bringing back the clay pot! Apparently he had been unable to find a place in the sky to leave the sickness container.

While Snipe was still a short distance above the earth, the clay pot slipped from his grasp and fell to the ground. The clay pot burst, and sickness scattered to all parts of the world again. Since that time, the people have not succeeded in their attempts to recapture the many kinds of sickness and put them back into a clay pot.

THE GREAT FLOOD

IN the old days, a young hunter once rescued a frog from a fire. He took the frog to his cabin in the village and fed the small creature while its burns healed.

Later the grateful frog said to his friend, "Water will soon cover all of the land. Make a raft and put a thick layer of grass underneath so the beavers cannot cut holes in the logs."

Frog's warnings alarmed the young man, so he made a large raft from long dry logs, putting grass underneath to protect the logs from beavers. Then he warned the other people in the village that a great flood would soon cover the land. But everyone just laughed at Frog's prediction and made fun of the man who was crazy enough to build such a huge raft far from deep water.

They didn't laugh very long, though, for soon the great flood came as Frog had warned. The builder of the raft assembled his family, Frog, and many other animals and birds on the clumsy boat. The water rose higher and higher. Soon the water covered first the trees and then the tallest mountains.

Many birds flew up to the sky and caught hold of it. Woodpecker got so high that the sun burned his head. That's why his feathers turned red. Since that time, Alabamas and Coushattas have called this bird Redheaded Woodpecker.

One bird with a long, slender tail caught hold of the sky, but the water rose higher and finally touched the bird's feathers, causing the tail feathers to divide and curl slightly. The people named this bird Scissor-Tail.

Part II

Origins of Animal
and Bird Characteristics

WHEN the world was new, the animals and birds could talk. They were friends of the Alabamas and Coushattas, and all lived together peacefully in a large village.

If something happened that should be discussed by all of the villagers, the old chief called the inhabitants to meet in council. On these occasions the creatures and people sat in assigned places around the square-ground. The chief and the other people occupied the eastern side of the square; the animals sat on the northern edge. The largest animals—Buffalo, Bear, and Panther—sat next to the people. The other animals, in order from the largest to the smallest, occupied the remaining area assigned to the animals.

The birds sat on the south side of the square, beginning with Eagle and Buzzard and extending down to the smaller birds. A few of the winged creatures—Whippoorwill, Wren, and Hummingbird—sat on the limb of a tree so they could see over the heads of their larger friends. The western side of the square was usually unoccupied.

The women of the village learned to make the various utensils and items of clothing used in their homes. Some excelled in making cane baskets, while others were more adept at shaping clay pots or in bead work.

One woman developed special skill in weaving moss blankets, and everyone liked her work with moss. She was called "Blanket Weaver."

Now, the secret of this woman's success was that she had learned to use color in her blankets. After she twisted moss into strands, she dyed the strands in pots of color—red, yellow and black—which she made from the bark and roots of certain trees. Then she hung the colored strands in a tree to dry. Afterward, she stored them in a cane basket in her cabin.

One day Blanket Weaver decided to begin work on a new blanket. When she took down her storage basket, however, she saw that the basket was empty.

She ran outside her house and cried out, "Someone has stolen my beautiful moss strands!"

The chief and other inhabitants of the village gathered around her. Blanker Weaver said, "For several days I have been twisting and coloring moss strands for a new blanket. I made enough to fill a basket.

While I was away from my house, a thief entered the cabin and stole all of them."

The villagers were shocked to hear that someone had stolen the strands. This was a terrible deed. Nothing like this had ever occurred since the beginning of their village.

The chief immediately called a council to decide what to do about the theft. All of the people, animals, and birds went to the square-ground and sat down in their assigned places.

Then the chief walked to a low mound in the square and said, "We have lived in this village as friends, and we have always trusted each other. No one has ever stolen anything from his neighbor. But today we discovered that a thief is among us."

The old man stopped talking for a brief period as the villagers sat in a stunned silence, thinking about the words of the chief.

"Someone in this village is a thief," the chief continued. "Only a resident of this village could know that Blanket Weaver had a basket of beautiful moss strands. Also, only we around this square would know when to enter Blanket Weaver's cabin to steal the strands."

Immediately the people said, "We didn't steal them."

Then the animals shouted, "We are not thieves. We didn't take the strands."

Finally, the birds denied the theft. But when all of the creatures and people were quiet again, Wren said, "Whippoorwill didn't say anything. He is just sitting here with his head under his wing."

The chief walked over to Whippoorwill, looked at him closely, and said, "Whippoorwill is the thief. He shows by his actions that he is guilty."

"Yes, you are right," admitted Whippoorwill. "My heart will always feel sorry if I do not confess that I stole from Blanket Weaver. I entered the cabin through the smoke-hole and took the moss strands from her basket."

The villagers decided to punish Whippoorwill, so the chief pronounced the punishment as follows: "From now on Whippoorwill cannot talk in our language. All he can say is 'I stole it,' so everyone will always know he is a thief."

Whippoorwill was so ashamed of himself that he decided to leave the village and make his home in the thick underbrush somewhere in the woods. He still lives in isolated places, and if you listen carefully near a creek or river, you can hear him saying, "I stole it. I stole it."

WHY TURTLE'S SHELL IS DIVIDED INTO SQUARES

ONE DAY Turtle went walking through the woods. As he wandered around, he saw some ants struggling with a large stone which had become dislodged and had closed the entrance to their home. The little creatures were trying to move the stone from their doorway. Turtle removed the stone and thereby gained the friendship of the ants.

As Turtle continued his walk, he approached a clearing in the forest. Here he saw Fox and Wolf arguing as to which could run faster. Turtle, in an effort to make peace, jokingly said that he was faster than either of them. The high-tempered Fox then challenged Turtle to run a race with him.

Now, Turtle knew that he was slower than Fox—but he knew also that he would be the laughingstock of the forest if he failed to make good his boast. There was nothing he could do but accept the challenge. They agreed that, three days later, they would race over three hills just beyond the field in which they were talking.

Turtle asked three of his tortoise friends to help him win the race. He gave each of them a white feather to wear on the day of the race. The first friend hid near the top of the second hill on the side nearest the starting point. The second tortoise took a similar position near the top of the third hill, and the third hid in some bushes near the finish line.

On the day of the race, Turtle put a white feather behind his ear and took his position beside Fox at the foot of the first hill. Redheaded Woodpecker gave the starting signal by drumming on a dead tree, and Fox leaped ahead. When the fleet animal was halfway up the first hill, Turtle ran into the woods near the starting point.

Fox quickly reached the top of the first hill, where he saw a tortoise with a white feather run over the top of the second hill and pass from sight. The second tortoise then hid in the nearby woods.

Unaware that Turtle was playing a trick on him, Fox began running faster. Soon he reached the top of the second hill, but when he looked ahead, he saw a tortoise with a white feather go over the third hill and drop out of sight.

Fox increased his pace and speedily reached the top of the third hill. From this point he could see the finish line. There, to his disappointment, was a tortoise with a white feather waiting for him. Fox was very much ashamed of himself, and he did not finish the race. He went into the nearby woods to hide.

Here he found another tortoise with a white feather behind his ear. Fox then realized that he had been tricked. He was so angry that he tore Turtle's shell into small squares. Soon, however, the ants came by and saw Turtle. They remembered that Turtle had once helped them, so they set to work and quickly repaired Turtle's shell. But their patch-work was so crude that the squares remain visible to this day.

WHY OPOSSUM'S TAIL IS BARE

LONG AGO Opossum had a long, bushy tail. He used to walk around in the forest and brag about it.

At that time Skunk had a slender and bare tail. Opossum would follow Skunk, laughing and saying, "Skunk's tail is scraped; my tail is bushy."

Skunk became quite angry and decided to play a trick on Opossum. He asked Opossum if he planned to attend a big dance in the village the next night.

"Of course I will be there," said Opossum. "I want to dance in the middle of the square-ground so everyone can see my beautiful tail."

Then Skunk went to his friend Cricket and said to him, "Opossum called me 'scraped tail,' and I need your help to play a trick on him."

Cricket agreed to assist, and Skunk gave him these directions: "Go to his house tomorrow morning and pretend to dress his tail for the dance that night. Cut it off, and I will exchange tails with him."

In the morning Cricket went to Opossum's house and said he would prepare his beautiful bushy tail for the dance. Opossum was pleased by this offer of assistance, so he lay down on a cane platform. Cricket pretended to comb his tail, but all the time he was gnawing it in such a manner that Opossum did not know what was happening.

When Cricket had cut off Opossum's tail, Skunk exchanged his bare tail for Opossum's bushy appendage and ran off with his prize. Cricket tied Skunk's tail onto Opossum and wrapped it in deerskin.

"The wrapping will keep your tail smooth," explained Cricket to Opossum. "Do not remove the deerskin until the dance begins tonight."

That night all the animals went to the square-ground for the big dance. When Opossum walked out in front of the crowd to begin dancing, he removed the wrapping from his tail. As he started dancing, all the animals around him began to laugh. Opossum thought they were enjoying his dancing, so he danced faster. The spectators laughed louder, and Opossum wondered what was so funny.

He looked down at his tail and was surprised to see that it was bare, without a hair upon it! He was embarrassed and began grinning and drooling. Then he ran away from the dancers and climbed a nearby tree.

The animals picked up stones and threw them at Opossum. One of the stones hit him on the head, and Opossum fell from the limb on which he had been sitting. On his way to the ground, however, his tail wrapped around a limb and he hung there. Since that time Opossum has been able to swing from a limb by his tail.

THE STORY OF CROW

IN a dense forest a hunter lived with an only son and another boy, a poor orphan. Every time the hunter looked for game, he brought back only liver for the two boys to eat.

The hunter's son and the orphan grew tired of eating only liver, and they frequently discussed this problem. While the two boys talked one day, the orphan asked, "What does he do with the meat? When he goes hunting again, let's watch him secretly."

So, when the hunter started out, the boys followed him. As they traveled along, the hunter killed a deer, most of which he carried with him. When the hunter came to the shore of a big lake, he called loudly. Instantly a bullfrog came out. When the bullfrog began eating the meat which the hunter placed on the shore, it turned into a beautiful woman. After the woman had eaten the meat, however, she changed back into a bullfrog and jumped into the lake. Quietly the young observers turned around and went home, arriving there ahead of the hunter, who did not suspect that the two boys had followed him.

The next day the two boys slipped away from the house and went to the big lake. After they called, the bullfrog came to the shore. The boys then killed the bullfrog with blowguns.

When the hunter came to feed the bullfrog later that day, he found it on the shore, pierced by two blowgun arrows which he recognized as belonging to his son and the orphan. The hunter immediately went to the nearest village and asked the chief to call a council meeting. When the villagers had assembled at the square-ground, the hunter said to them, "My son and an orphan have killed a person. They should be put to death." The people agreed, and the chief said that four warriors would go with the hunter to kill the boys next morning.

The two boys arrived at the village square-ground in time to hear the discussion of plans for their execution. They hurried home and collected many stinging insects—bumblebees, wasps, and hornets. The boys put the insects in large gourds. Then, near their cabin they dug a hole in which they planned to hide.

Early the next morning, the boys stationed some of their friends as pickets to watch for the men coming from the village. Hummingbirds formed the outermost row of guards, ducks were in the second group, and redheaded woodpeckers lined up in the third row. The boys placed quails in the fourth row, which was near the hole they had dug for a hiding place.

Hummingbirds were stationed farthest out because they are so swift and could warn the boys as soon as the men appeared. Ducks were next because they make loud noises as they pass overhead. Redheaded woodpeckers, in the third row, could fly to the tops of dead trees nearby to warn the boys by pecking on the dry wood. Quails formed the last row of sentinels because they make a noise with their wings when they fly.

In a short while, hummingbirds flew by to tell the boys that the hunter and four warriors were coming through the woods toward the cabin. Then the ducks flew over to warn that the men were nearer. Soon the redheaded woodpeckers began drumming on the dead trees. Finally, the quails flew up with a thundering noise, and the boys knew the men had arrived.

They broke the gourds filled with stinging insects. Next, they jumped into the hole they had dug and covered themselves with a deerskin. The insects stung the men until they killed all of them.

Later, when the boys came out of the hole, they saw the dead men lying near the cabin. Among the others they found the body of the hunter. While the boys stood nearby, a rather large bird emerged from the body of the hunter.

"From now on you shall travel about under the name 'Crow,' " said the orphan to the bird. Crow cawed and went flying out of sight. This was the beginning of Crow.

A RACE BETWEEN CRANE AND HUMMINGBIRD

HUMMINGBIRD flew around Crane one day and made some insulting remarks about Crane's lack of speed. They began arguing, and Crane became quite angry.

"I can fly faster than you," shouted the big bird.

"You are too big to fly fast," retorted Hummingbird.

After they had argued for some time, Crane finally said, "All right. Let's stop talking and see who is faster. Let's race to the ocean. The one who wins shall have his home near the water forever."

Hummingbird quickly accepted this challenge. He felt sure that he would win, since he was so swift—almost like a flash of lightning—and Crane was so heavy and slow.

At the starting signal Hummingbird darted away and was out of sight in a moment. He flew all day and at evening was far ahead of his rival. That night Hummingbird went to sleep perched on a limb of a tree.

Crane flew steadily all night long and passed Hummingbird about midnight. He was making so much noise flapping his wings, however, that he woke Hummingbird. The smaller bird then began flying and soon passed Crane.

On the second night, Hummingbird went to sleep roosting on the highest limb of another tree. Again Crane made so much noise flapping his wings that he disturbed Hummingbird, who flew swiftly by and left Crane out of sight.

On the third night, Crane decided that he wouldn't awaken his rival. When he drew near the tree in which Hummingbird was sleeping, Crane flew very high and just sailed along without flapping his wings until he was far ahead of the smaller bird. In this manner he reached the ocean before Hummingbird. And this is how Crane won the right to live around rivers, lakes, and marshes.

WHY TURTLE HAS RED EYES

ONE DAY some wolves started chasing a fawn. After a while the fawn became exhausted, so it jumped and lodged far up in the fork of a hickory nut tree.

The wolves didn't know how to get the fawn down. They just ran around the tree aimlessly.

Later that day Turtle was traveling through the forest and found the wolves holding a council.

"What are you talking about?" asked Turtle.

"A fawn is in this tree, and we are trying to get it down," replied one of the wolves.

Turtle said he would help them, and he shot the fawn with his bow and arrow.

Then the chief of the wolves asked, "Which part of the fawn do you want? Do you like the leg? Or would you prefer a shoulder?"

"No, I don't want those parts," answered Turtle.

The wolf asked if Turtle wanted another part of the fawn. Turtle said he didn't want any of the animal.

All of the wolves got on the carcass and in a short time devoured it completely. When the wolves departed, Turtle decided to play a trick on his wife. So he got some blood and wrapped layer after layer of leaves around it. He put this big roll on his back and went home. Turtle said to his wife, "This big roll is venison."

His wife untied the bundle but saw only leaves. "It is nothing," she said.

"Go farther in," instructed Turtle.

When she looked again, she found some blood, but nothing more. She became quite angry and threw the blood into Turtle's eyes. That is why Turtle's eyes are red.

WHY OPOSSUM CARRIES HER CHILDREN IN A POUCH

WHILE Opossum was away from her children one day, Bat picked them up and carried them to a hole in the rocks. So Opossum went about crying, not knowing how to rescue her children.

Origins of Animal and Bird Characteristics   19

Presently Raccoon asked, "Why are you crying?"

"I am crying because Bat has stolen my children and has taken them to a hole in the rocks," replied Opossum.

Then Raccoon said, "Guide me to the place."

So Opossum guided Raccoon to the hole in the rocks, and he went inside the cave. The darkness frightened him, however, and he ran out immediately and left Opossum.

Opossum continued crying until Rabbit said to her, "Why are you crying?"

"I am crying because Bat has taken my children from me and has hidden them in a hole in the rocks," answered Opossum.

"Show me the place," said Rabbit.

Opossum guided him to the hole in the rocks, and Rabbit went inside. But he, too, became scared and ran out. "I can't help you," he said.

While Opossum walked about crying continuously, Wolf said, "Show me Bat's cave."

When Opossum pointed out the hole in the rocks, Wolf went inside. When he found the little opossums, he grasped the babies and started out with them. Bat tried to stop him but could not.

When Wolf returned the young animals to their mother, he cut Opossum's skin to form a pouch and said to her, "Before your children have stopped nursing, keep them here; after they have stopped nursing, let them go."

Opossum has done so ever since.

WHY THE CATFISH HAS A FLAT HEAD

THE oldest men say that once the catfish chief called a council of all the catfish in a big river. When the catfish had gathered near a sunken log, the chief said to them, "A big buffalo comes to the edge of this river to drink water and eat grass. He disturbs us when we search for food in the shallow water. I think we should wait for him at sunset today and kill him."

All of the other catfish said they thought this was a good thing to do. They agreed to meet at a designated place at sunset that day.

The buffalo came to the river's edge three times during the day. On these occasions the catfish did not bother him, since the big animal could easily see them in the shallow water. But when he appeared after sunset, the catfish were ready for him. A large number of them had assembled at the place where the buffalo usually waded in the water. They hid in the grass near the river's edge.

The buffalo walked into the river and began drinking. Then one of the biggest catfish swam rapidly toward him and stuck his spear into the animal's leg.

The startled buffalo looked down to see what caused the pain in his leg. As he did so, he saw the multitude of catfish in the water. He began to trample them with his hooves.

The buffalo's crushing blows forced some of the catfish into the soft mud. These fish still carry spears, but their heads are flat from the time when the buffalo trampled them into the mud with his hooves.

Part III

Afterworld Trip

A JOURNEY TO THE SKY

LONG AGO three little boys lived near each other in a village. Every day these boys played together. While they were playing one day, they made plans to travel to the end of the world when they grew up.

As the years passed, and the boys grew to be young men, they still remembered their plan to travel to the end of the world. They continued to talk about this trip and, meeting one afternoon near the village square-ground, decided to start their journey the next morning.

Just as the sun rose, they picked up their deerskin bags and started out. Each bag contained a blanket and food. Also, they carried knives, bows and arrows for protection, because their path would lead them through dense forests full of wild animals.

The young men decided to travel with the sun. Had they gone toward the east, the sun would have been too hot. They reasoned that the sun, as it approached the place where it disappeared from earth, already would have used its heat during the day.

On the second day, they saw a wild turkey perched on the limb of a tall tree. The first traveler brought the turkey down with an arrow. When the travelers went forward to get the fowl, however, they found only a dead mosquito with an arrow lying across its back. This discovery caused them great surprise; they could think of no explanation for this event.

They resumed their journey and soon encountered a black bear, which immediately became a black hairy caterpillar. This transformation seemed miraculous, but they had no time to investigate.

A few days later a huge eagle attacked the three young men. The eagle was a good fighter, but he couldn't whip three men. One of them plunged a long knife into the heart of the eagle.

Eventually the men approached the edge of a wide plain. In the distance they saw a mountain standing in their path. Several days elapsed before they reached the mountain, and behold! it was only a small land tortoise crawling across the plain. By this time, they were no longer astonished: the inexplicable had ceased to surprise them.

After they crossed the plain, the travelers entered a dark forest where many rattlesnakes lived—so many that there seemed to be one rattlesnake for each step they took. To protect their legs, they stripped bark from a slippery elm tree and made leggings. Snakes by the thousands attacked them until the elm bark was in shreds and appeared like hair on their legs.

So many strange things had happened by now that they grew cautious as they approached what appeared from a distance to be a great patch of blue sky near the earth. As they drew nearer, they could see a body of water so wide that the opposite shore was out of sight. There seemed no way to cross this ocean.

When the three friends had almost abandoned hope of continuing their journey, an enormous Snake-Crawfish (Horned Snake) approached the shore. This snake was as large around as a tree trunk, with horns on his head and scales that glittered like sparks of fire. Alternating red, yellow, and black rings covered the awesome creature's body.

The men started looking in their food bags. All they found was half of a small animal they had cooked that morning. One of the men threw a bone to the edge of the water. When Horned Snake came for the bone, the travelers jumped on his back. They threw another bone a short distance from the shore, and Horned Snake immediately swam toward it.

After Horned Snake had finished the second bone, one of the adventurers threw another bone farther ahead. Soon Horned Snake swam toward the third bone. They continued in this way until they approached the opposite shore. Only one bone remained, and the strongest man was selected to throw it. This man braced himself and threw the bone to the edge of the water. The great Horned Snake made his way to the shore, and the travelers dismounted and thanked Horned Snake for the ride. But the big creature didn't realize that he had been tricked. He had only been looking for something to eat; yet he had carried the three men across the ocean.

The years went by, and the adventurers became old men with gray beards on their chins. They did not lose hope; to the contrary, they continued walking with enthusiasm. One day they heard a noise so far away that they could barely hear it. Two huge objects seemed to be clashing together at regular intervals. As they journeyed, the noise grew louder, and they realized that each day they were approaching a great conflict of some sort.

The noise became so loud that the men were almost deafened. Finally, they walked out of a dense forest, and in the distance they saw a startling phenomenon: over and over, the sky would fall, strike the earth, and then go up again. When the sky made its upward movement, there was an open space between the earth and sky. Almost immediately the sky fell again, producing a dull thud. This swinging action was repeated at intervals so that it seemed an eternal combat raged between the earth and sky.

While the adventurers watched this great contest, the fact dawned on them that they had come to the end of the earth. They forgot their other experiences as they watched the sky hitting the earth.

When the men began to recover from their amazement, the first traveler suggested that they could run under the sky as it made its upward movement. He said that after going across they would be in a new world and could continue their explorations. The second traveler agreed, but the third traveler was afraid to make the attempt.

As the sky came down and then went up, the first two men ran to the other side. The third traveler saw that his friends had crossed safely; and since he knew that he could not return alone through the thick woods, he decided to go across, also. But he waited too long to start. When he was halfway across, the sky came down again and crushed him.

The two remaining adventurers jumped on the sky as it went up. After a swift journey into space, they reached the beautiful country of another world. What they saw held them spellbound. Every kind of bird and beast roamed contentedly through the forests and over the meadows. People lived together peacefully, and hatred and suffering were unknown. Indeed, conditions were so nearly perfect that the travelers could not fully describe later what they had seen.

As the two friends wandered from place to place, they were warned not to touch any of the animals or any of the people. By accident, however, one traveler touched a horse, which immediately turned into a skeleton. The other traveler touched a young boy, who also became a skeleton. The adventurers then realized that this new world contained only the spirits of animals and people who once had lived on earth.

After the travelers completed their investigation of this strange land, they were given seeds of plants that produced such foods as watermelons, beans, potatoes, and barley. Then Aba Mikko, the Great Chief, invited them to sleep in a beautiful house. When the travelers awoke the following morning, they found that they were back in the same log cabins they had lived in before starting their journey.

Since the two friends were now very old, the people of the village did not immediately recognize them. But eventually some of the oldest men and women remembered them. The travelers recounted their experiences and distributed the seeds among their friends. Thus began the cultivation of several new food plants.

Part IV

Trickster Cycle

THE BUFFALO TUG-OF-WAR

DURING a long journey through the woods one day, Rabbit saw some buffalo tracks in the sand. Soon he overtook a large buffalo that was walking toward a low hill.

Rabbit was tired of his uneventful trip, so he decided to create a little excitement. He said to Buffalo, "People are always talking about how strong you are. I am small, but I believe I am stronger than you. Let's get a grapevine and see who can pull the other across a mark on top of that hill ahead of us."

Buffalo was amused by this challenge, but he agreed to Rabbit's plan for a trial of strength.

Rabbit said, "I will bring a vine, and when you feel me jerk it, you begin pulling."

Then Rabbit went over the hill and made the same arrangement with another buffalo he found there. Next, he got a grapevine and carried an end to the first buffalo and took the other end of the vine across the hill to the second buffalo. He made a mark on top of the hill to see which could pull the other across.

Rabbit stationed himself in the middle, out of sight of the two beasts, and jerked the vine. The two buffalo began pulling, each thinking that Rabbit was at the other end. Each in turn pulled the other near the mark; then the other would drag him back.

The big animals pulled against each other until they were amazed at Rabbit's strength. They decided to find out how Rabbit was pulling so hard, so each walked slowly up the hill, pulling all the while, and gradually reached the top, where Rabbit was hiding. There the buffalo saw each other but no Rabbit at all, for he had run away when he saw them coming up the hill.

After talking it over, the buffalo agreed that Rabbit should not be allowed to drink any more water. So the word went out to all the other buffalo, who control the water, that Rabbit should not be allowed to drink water because of his deception.

Day after day, as Rabbit went to drink, the buffalo ordered him away. Finally he made a plan to fool the buffalo. He found the skin of a fawn and, putting it on, he approached a small lake and began bleating like a young fawn in distress.

A buffalo heard the cry and asked why he cried.

"Because Rabbit says the buffalo have forbidden all animals to drink any more water," said the disguised Rabbit.

"He has lied," said the buffalo. "It is only Rabbit who cannot drink any more. You can always get all the water you want."

So Rabbit drank and, later, he bragged to his friends about how he had deceived the big buffalo.

RABBIT AND THE TURKEYS

RABBIT saw some turkeys in the woods and began thinking about how he could capture the big birds. He knew that turkeys are curious about things they do not understand. So Rabbit took a large deerskin bag to the top of a hill near the turkeys. Then he got into the bag and began rolling down. As he rolled along, Rabbit laughed loudly and pretended to enjoy his activity.

The turkeys walked to the bottom of the hill and watched Rabbit as he played. After Rabbit had rolled down the hill three times, one of the turkeys asked, "Why are you rolling down the hill in that bag?"

"Because I am having so much fun," answered Rabbit.

"You are lying," accused the turkey.

"Try it if you don't believe me," replied Rabbit. "Suppose one of you rolls down the hill in the bag."

One of the turkeys got into the bag and rolled down, laughing and saying, "Yes, this is fun. I like to play this way."

Then all of the turkeys got into the bag and rolled down. When they arrived at the bottom of the hill, Rabbit fastened the top of the bag. In this manner he captured the foolish birds.

Rabbit carried the turkeys to his grandmother, who put the birds in a log hut. But the grandmother failed to block the smoke-hole of the hut, and a few days later all but one of the turkeys escaped.

Now, Rabbit was very selfish, so he made a plan with which he hoped to deceive his grandmother. If Rabbit's plan worked, his grandmother would cook the remaining turkey but would not eat any of it.

Rabbit pretended to be very angry at the loss of the other turkeys and said to his grandmother, "I wanted to prepare a turkey feast for

a large number of people. Since only one turkey is left, cook it, and I
will invite only a few people."

Then he went away and walked around for a while. When he returned
to the cabin, he said to his grandmother, "The people are coming."

Although Rabbit said that his guests were arriving, it was he himself
who talked in such a way as to convey the impression that several
people were approaching the cabin. After his grandmother placed the
cooked turkey on a cane platform and left the room, Rabbit said, "All
is ready. Let us eat."

Rabbit jumped upon the platform in one place and then in another.
He ate the food and made a continuous noise like several people talking
and eating.

The grandmother in the adjoining room believed that her grandson
and several guests were present to enjoy the meal, but it was Rabbit
alone who ate all the turkey meat.

WHY RABBIT HAS BIG EYES AND LONG EARS

DURING one of his trips through the forest, Rabbit met Raccoon,
and the two became good friends. While they were talking one day,
Raccoon noticed that Rabbit was wearing very beautiful shoes. Rabbit
then proudly said, "My shoes are so good that the cold wind can not
get through to my feet. When I run along in them through the woods,
the briars do not hurt me. And, when I have my shoes on, the girls
look at my feet."

Raccoon wanted Rabbit's shoes, so he said, "Let us swap. Will you
exchange them for a woman?"

But Rabbit said, "Let me see the woman first."

"Tomorrow night I will have a dance, and you come there and see
the girl," invited Raccoon.

Next day Rabbit was very happy, and that night he set out to the
dance, shouting and singing as he went. When he arrived, he found
Raccoon had invited everyone to be present.

Now Rabbit wanted very much to deceive Raccoon, so he put on
rotten moccasins and sat down in the dark near the edge of the crowd.
"Where is the woman?" asked Rabbit, talking to Raccoon.

The latter answered, "I will give you the one in the middle of the circle if you will let me have your shoes in exchange."

Following his plan to deceive Raccoon, Rabbit then said, "Bring the woman in the dark, and I will pull my shoes off and give them to you. But do not wear the shoes tonight. Instead, wait until tomorrow before putting them on."

So Raccoon brought his daughter to Rabbit and said, "This is your wife; take her with you." After giving the rotten moccasins to Raccoon, Rabbit took the woman and went away with her.

Rabbit loved this woman and kept looking at her. He looked at her so much that he soon began winking his eyes. As a result, his eyes grew big and his ears grew long, remaining that way to this day.

RABBIT OUTWITS A FARMER

ONE warm summer day a farmer was hoeing peas in his field. The peas had just sprouted and were barely tall enough to be hoed. As the farmer finished one row and stood in the shade to rest, Rabbit came along and asked, "What are you doing in this field?"

The farmer answered, "I have been hoeing peas so that I will have something to eat when cold weather comes."

"If you were like me," taunted Rabbit, "you wouldn't have to work at all but would always have a good time." Then he went merrily on his way.

Some time later, when the peas were almost ripe, Rabbit returned to the field. The farmer was away, so Rabbit decided to play a trick on him. Accordingly, he cut down every plant in the field and went back into the forest.

When the farmer returned to his field, he saw that his crop was ruined. He found the tracks of a small animal in the field, so he suspected that Rabbit had cut down the peas.

The next day the farmer met Rabbit in the forest, and he asked why Rabbit had destroyed the crop of peas. Rabbit replied, "I thought you told me that I could have the peas when they grew up."

"You know that is not true," accused the farmer. "I will kill you when I catch you."

Rabbit said, "I will let you kill me only if you will do it by chopping off my head."

The farmer agreed, and Rabbit told him to get a battle-axe. Rabbit then laid his head on a large stone.

The farmer said to himself, "Now I will get revenge for the destruction of my crop. I will swing the axe so hard that it will go right through Rabbit's neck."

Accordingly, he swung the axe with all his force. But before the axe descended, Rabbit jumped out of the way. The sharp axe hit the stone and broke into many pieces. The farmer was so angry that he started to turn his dogs loose to kill Rabbit. He abandoned the plan, though, when Rabbit said he would set the woods on fire if the farmer tried to kill him on land in any way besides the method they had agreed upon.

Rabbit then suggested another way in which the farmer could get revenge. Rabbit said he could be killed only by drowning. So the farmer put him in a basket with a large stone, threw the basket over his shoulder, and started toward the sea.

For a long time the farmer walked without stopping. Finally, Rabbit asked how much farther they would have to travel before they reached the sea. The farmer said that the sea was now in sight.

Rabbit then suggested, "You had better get a drink of water, because you have walked all day without stopping."

The farmer agreed that he really was thirsty. He laid the basket down and walked to a nearby spring for a drink.

While the farmer was away, another man came along, driving some cattle, and asked Rabbit why he was in the basket. Rabbit said that someone was taking him to the home of the chief, who had given him his daughter. He said that he could not be seen by anyone until he married the chief's daughter. That was the reason he was in a basket.

Now, the stranger had seen the chief's daughter, and he admired her, so he asked to take Rabbit's place. Rabbit told him to unfasten the top of the basket and jump into it. He did so, and Rabbit stepped out and drove the cattle away.

When the farmer returned from the spring, he carried the basket to the seashore. Without hesitating he threw the weighted basket into the water.

On the following day the farmer met Rabbit, who was driving a herd of cattle. To the farmer's inquiries Rabbit replied, "When someone is thrown into the sea but swims to the shore, that indicates that he will have good luck. That is why I have a herd of cattle."

The farmer asked, "If I were thrown into the sea, would I, too, have good luck when I come out of the water?"

"Yes, you will," said Rabbit. To the farmer's mind came visions of good crops and an abundance of food. So he got into a basket and asked Rabbit to carry him to the sea. From a cliff overlooking the sea, Rabbit threw the farmer into the water, which closed forever over the gullible man.

RABBIT PLAYS PRANKS ON BIG MAN-EATER

LONG AGO, before the days of our oldest grandfathers, people and all the small animals lived on one side of a small stream. Big Man-Eaters lived on the opposite side. At regular intervals, Big Man-Eaters crossed over to kill people.

Those who escaped held councils on several occasions, but could not agree on a plan to destroy their enemies. Finally, Rabbit volunteered to stop the Big Man-Eaters from crossing the stream.

While Rabbit walked through the forest three days later, he met a Big Man-Eater. They started talking, and Rabbit described a beautiful country on the other side of some distant hills. He painted such an interesting word picture of the region that Big Man-Eater said he wanted to see this wonderful country. Rabbit then offered to guide him to it, and they began their journey.

All day Rabbit and Big Man-Eater traveled through the forest. After sunset they made camp at a place which Rabbit called "The Place of Hot Ashes." They built a big fire and prepared a spot to sleep. As they were about to lie down, Rabbit said, "How loud do you snore when you are really asleep?"

"My friends say that I usually snore low and fast when I am half asleep, but when I am really asleep, I snore loud and slow," answered Big Man-Eater. "How loud do you snore?"

"I snore so low that you cannot tell whether I am asleep or awake," replied Rabbit.

They both lay down, and Rabbit immediately pretended to be

asleep. Soon Big Man-Eater began snoring, low and fast at first, and then loud and slow. When the snoring became very loud and very slow, Rabbit threw some cold ashes on himself and some hot ashes on Big Man-Eater. The ashes burned the big animal painfully, and he rolled around on the ground.

Rabbit pretended that the ashes burned him, also. He said that the territory on which they camped had been an unbearable country for a long time. After he had spent the entire night nursing his painful burns, Big Man-Eater said he was ready to believe this statement.

Early the next morning they resumed their journey. As they walked along, Rabbit would push each dead tree. If the tree was strong, he would say, "This is not a good camping place because the tree is weak and might fall on us."

Finally, they approached a dead tree that apparently was about to fall. Rabbit, however, walked to the tree, gave it a little push, and said, "This tree is strong and will not fall on us." Accordingly, they prepared to spend the night near the base of the dead tree.

When Big Man-Eater started snoring loud and slow, Rabbit pushed the dead tree, causing it to fall on the big animal. Since Rabbit lay down on the ground and started rolling around and groaning, Big Man-Eater thought that Rabbit, too, had been asleep when the tree fell.

On the third day Rabbit directed their journey so that they circled back to the small stream which separated the Big Man-Eaters from the people and small animals. Rabbit said, "Let us jump across to see which is the better jumper. You jump first."

Big Man-Eater, however, wanted Rabbit to be the first jumper. Rabbit then said, "We shall jump at the same time."

They agreed that Rabbit should give the signal. He did so, and jumped first. When Big Man-Eater had also jumped across the stream, Rabbit quickly jumped back across and sang a magic song. Instantly the little stream widened into an ocean. Since then people and small animals have been separated from Big Man-Eaters by a great ocean.

RABBIT was so boastful that he would claim to do whatever he saw anyone else do. He antagonized all the other animals by bragging constantly about his deeds.

The animals held a secret council to decide how to silence Rabbit. They talked about several plans to accomplish this purpose.

"Let's deceive Rabbit by sending him into the forest to get a rattlesnake," suggested the chief. "Perhaps the snake will bite him and Rabbit will die."

The others agreed to try this plan, so the chief sent for Rabbit. "We talked about making you leave the village," said the chief, "but we finally decided to let you live here if you can prove that you are a good hunter. Go into the forest and bring back a large rattlesnake."

Rabbit was so deceitful that he always suspected the worst in others. Now he believed that the chief was playing a trick on him. After Rabbit left the village on his assignment to catch a rattlesnake, he broke off a long stick, sharpened it, and used it as a walking stick.

When Rabbit found a rattlesnake, he said to him, "Some of my friends in the village said that Rattlesnake is long, and others said that you are short. So I agreed to measure you to settle the argument."

Rabbit, of course, was telling a lie, but Rattlesnake did not know it. He agreed to Rabbit's plan for a measurement and stretched out on the ground.

Rabbit began measuring Rattlesnake with his stick, starting at the snake's tail and working toward his head. When Rabbit had nearly finished his job of measuring, he ran his sharp stick through Rattlesnake's head and killed him. Then Rabbit put his stick over his shoulder with the snake impaled on it and went back to the village.

"We wanted the snake alive," said the chief. "He is no good now. Throw him away." So Rabbit threw the dead snake into the forest.

Then the chief said to him, "Take this sack and bring it back full of wasps."

Near the village Rabbit found a large wasps' nest, and he said to the winged creatures, "My friends in the village told me that there are so few of you that you cannot fill this sack, but I said you could. Who is correct?"

"We will fill the sack," said the wasps. To prove that they were very numerous they flew into the sack. When it was full of wasps, Rabbit tied it up and carried it to the village.

The chief decided that Rabbit should be tested further, and he said to Rabbit, "Kill an alligator and bring it here. When I see it, I will let you know whether or not you may live in the village."

Rabbit started toward a river thinking about how he would get Alligator to come out of the water so he could kill him. When he arrived at the river, Rabbit called, "Alligator, are you there?"

Alligator poked his head above the water and said, "Yes, I am here. What do you want?"

"The chief sent me to ask you to help us move a log to our square-ground," replied Rabbit. "We are trying to provide more seats for our meetings there."

"All right," said Alligator, "I will help you move the log."

The big creature came out of the water and walked with Rabbit toward the village. When they had almost reached the square-ground, Rabbit picked up a club and hit his companion in order to kill him. He hit Alligator repeatedly on his back, but Alligator ran to the river and jumped into the water.

Rabbit thought, "Alligator won't believe anything I say now. How can I get him to come out of the river again?" He reflected upon the best means of deceiving Alligator, and finally decided to use this plan: he killed a fawn, skinned it, and tied the skin to his back so that he looked like a fawn. Then he returned to the river and called Alligator again.

Alligator came to the surface and saw what appeared to be a little fawn standing near the water's edge. "Why have you come here?" asked Alligator.

The disguised Rabbit replied, "The chief wants you to move a log to our square-ground. He sent Rabbit to tell you this, but he has not returned. I came to see what happened to him."

"Rabbit came here to ask me to help, and then he beat me," said Alligator. Nevertheless, he agreed again to move a log to the square-ground. He came out of the water, and the two started through the forest toward the village.

As they walked along, Alligator said, "Near here is the place where Rabbit beat me."

"Did he hurt you badly?" asked Rabbit, who was still wearing the fawn's skin.

"Yes," replied Alligator, "but he did not hit me in a dangerous place. If he had hit me in the head, he would have killed me."

This was the information Rabbit needed to carry out his scheme. Presently he hit the unsuspecting Alligator in the head with a club and killed him. Then he dragged Alligator to the village.

When he brought Alligator's body to the chief, the latter said, "You have earned the right to live in the village but you must stay away from the lodges." So he picked up Rabbit and threw him into some grass and bushes on the edge of the village. Rabbit has made his home there since that time.

THE BUNGLING HOST

IN the old days, Bear and Rabbit were friends. One day, as they walked across a field, Bear said to Rabbit, "Come and smoke tobacco with me tomorrow afternoon. I live in that red house over there."

At the appointed time, Rabbit went to Bear's house, which was a hollow tree.

"Come in and sit down," said Bear. So Rabbit sat down, and the two friends smoked and talked for a while.

Bear called his wife and said, "Let's have beans for dinner. My friend likes beans."

"I need grease to cook beans, and I don't have any," said Bear's wife.

"Don't worry about it. I will get some grease," Bear assured her.

So he cut a gash in his side, and out ran the grease. His wife put the grease in a pot with some beans. After the beans had cooked, they had a fine dinner and later smoked tobacco again.

When Rabbit was preparing to go home, he said, "Come and visit me tomorrow."

"Where do you live?" asked Bear.

"I live in the white house on the other side of this field," replied Rabbit.

"All right," said Bear, "I will be there."

On the next day, Bear went to Rabbit's house, which was made of dried white grass. Rabbit told Bear to come in and sit down. So Bear sat down, and they talked.

Later, Rabbit called his wife and told her to prepare some beans for dinner.

"We don't have any grease for cooking," said Rabbit's wife.

"Well, I know how to get some," said Rabbit. Then he got a knife and tried to cut a gash in his side. On the second attempt the knife went deep into his side. Rabbit screamed and fell on the ground.

"I am the only one who can get grease that way," said Bear. "You have hurt yourself."

He hurried outside to look for a doctor. Along the way Bear saw a turkey buzzard. He said to the big bird. "Rabbit cut himself, and I am looking for someone to treat him."

"I make medicine," said Buzzard. "I can take care of Rabbit." So Bear led Buzzard to Rabbit's house.

"When I treat an injured person, I don't want anyone else in the house to disturb me," said Buzzard. "Also, you must make the smoke-hole in this house bigger so I will have more light."

Raccoon and several other friends of Rabbit had gathered outside the house. They followed Buzzard's directions and enlarged the smoke-hole. Then they shut Buzzard up in the house with Rabbit.

Buzzard began working, and Rabbit screamed in agony. Bear, who was sitting outside the door, asked, "What is happening?"

"I am just cleaning the place where Rabbit cut himself," said Buzzard.

Again Rabbit screamed, but Buzzard said, "Rabbit cries out because he is afraid of the medicine."

Rabbit continued screaming, but not so loudly as at first, and after a while he stopped. Bear asked, "How is the patient?"

"He is better," said Buzzard. Presently he flew through the cabin's smoke-hole and lighted in a tree nearby.

"Rabbit is in the house waiting for you," Buzzard said to the animals standing near the door.

Bear opened the door and went inside. He found only a pile of bones on the ground where Rabbit had been lying.

Just then an orphan with a blowgun walked by, and Bear said to him, "We asked Buzzard to treat Rabbit, but he killed and ate our friend. Shoot at Buzzard and try to kill him."

Orphan shot several arrows at Buzzard and hit the vulture in the nose. The blowgun arrows were so small, however, that they only enlarged Buzzard's nostrils, making them as we see them today.

Buzzard said, "You have made a good breathing place for me." Then he flew away.

Part V

Adventures with Cannibals

OUTWITTING THE CANNIBALS

O NCE there were six brothers living near the edge of a village. Each day five of the brothers would go hunting, while the sixth stayed home to do the cooking. None of them liked to miss a chance to go hunting, so they took turns cooking.

One day the youngest brother was serving as cook. While he was washing some potatoes in a creek, he lost his balance and fell into the water. As he struggled beneath the surface of the creek, his hand touched a piece of wood. He carried the piece of wood to the bank of the creek, where he found that the wood was really a baby-board. And fastened to the board was a tiny little girl, still alive!

When the other brothers returned from their hunting trip, they all looked at the baby girl and felt sorry for her. Since no one came around asking about her, the brothers decided to keep the little girl with them. As she grew older, she learned to do all the cooking and housework, so all six of the brothers could go hunting at the same time.

While the brothers were out hunting one day, a strange person slipped into the house, killed the girl housekeeper, and paddled away in a canoe. The girl returned to life, however, and later told the brothers what had happened.

On the following day the men pretended to go hunting again. This time they doubled back on their trail and hid near their house.

As the brothers had expected, the stranger came back to the house. On a certain signal, the six brothers started shooting arrows into the stranger, who died instantly.

One of the brothers pushed the visitor's canoe into the creek, and it went down the stream until presently it began circling in one spot. This seemed unusual to the brothers, so one of them left to make an investigation—but he did not come back. Another soon followed—and he, too, did not return. A third went and did not return. Likewise, the fourth and fifth started out and failed to return.

Finally, the sixth departed to look for his brothers. At dinner time on the first day, he climbed into a persimmon tree and ate some of the fruit. While he was eating the persimmons, a female cannibal came along under the tree carrying a basket and a club. When she looked up and saw the man, she said, "The other men who climbed that tree wrestled with me. Get down and let's wrestle."

After the cannibal had laid the basket and the club on the ground, the hunter climbed down and began wrestling with her. Quickly she threw him down, but he got up immediately. This happened several times. Presently, she threw him down near her club, whereupon he seized the club and killed her.

He cut off her head with a hatchet, but the cannibal's head reunited with her body. He cut the head off again, and again the head went back onto the body. But the third time he cut off the head it remained severed.

When the cannibal was dead, the young hunter cut her to pieces and threw the parts away. He took her heart and hit a tree with it. "Stick there and become tree fungus," he said. He hung the intestines on a tree, and from that day they have been clinging to trees in the shape of long blue vines. After he put the woman's nose and her club in the basket, he set out along the path from which the cannibal had come.

Presently he approached some girls who were pounding corn with a pestle. When they saw the nose in the basket, they said, "That looks like our grandmother's nose."

"No," he explained, "it is a pipe which Aba Mikko sent me."

And they said of the club, "This is like our grandmother's club." But he said, "No, Aba Mikko sent it to me. It is to tickle people. If you will lie down in a straight line, I will show you how it works." Accordingly, they all lay down, and he cut their throats.

A little later he asked a small boy where the cannibals threw the bones of people they had eaten. "In that direction," the boy answered, pointing to a large tree. Beneath this tree the young man found many bones. Among them were his brothers'.

As he shot an arrow over one pile of bones, he said, "Look out! The arrow will stick into you." When he spoke these words, the dead brother awoke and sat up. Then the youngest brother shot an arrow over each of his other brothers until all had come to life.

"Don't look behind," he said to them. But, as they went along, one of them looked back, turned into a wildcat, and ran away growling. Another looked back, turned into a panther, and went off howling. The third looked back and turned into an alligator. In the same manner the fourth changed into an owl. Likewise, the fifth became a chicken hawk and flew away. The sixth brother returned home alone.

ONE DAY a young girl went down to a river to get some water. Here she saw a cannibal sitting in a canoe and holding up some little puppies. "Come here and look at them," invited the cannibal.

Since the young girl liked puppies, she stepped into the canoe for a closer look. As she did so, the cannibal untied the canoe and paddled quickly down the river to his house.

Next day the cannibal went hunting but didn't kill anything. When he came home, he said to the captive girl, "Cut off a piece of your body and roast it for me." But instead his wife cut off a piece of her own flesh and gave it to the girl, who roasted it for the cannibal's supper.

On the following day, while the cannibal was away on another hunting trip, his wife said to the young girl, "He has caused me grief by nearly eating me up. If you stay here, he will eat you, also. Run away."

Now, many trails began at the cannibal's house and led in all directions into the forest. To carry out the plan of escape the cannibal's wife suggested, the girl ran a short distance down one of these trails and returned to the house. Then she traveled along another trail awhile and returned to the house. In this manner she soon traveled a short distance along each of the trails leading from the cannibal's home, always taking care to conceal the footprints she made as she returned to the house.

Meanwhile, the cannibal's wife hid her husband's magic chunk stone. Then she gave the young girl three ripe huckleberries, three blackberries, three pieces of cane, and some mud.

"Run along this old trail," she instructed. "When you hear the cannibal chasing you, throw down the huckleberries and run on. The next time he almost catches you, throw down the blackberries. Likewise, later throw down the cane and then the mud."

When the cannibal arrived late that afternoon, he called the young girl. No one answered him. Again he called, and still there was no answer.

He suspected that she had run away, so he started looking for his chunk stone and finally found it after looking everywhere. He placed this magic roller on one trail, and it rolled a short distance and stopped. The cannibal then placed it on another trail, and again the stone stopped after rolling a short distance. In this manner, the cannibal rolled the stone a short distance along nearly all the trails leading from his house, trying to locate the trail along which his former captive had fled.

While the cannibal was searching for the right trail, the young girl traveled a long distance toward her house. Running across a meadow later in the afternoon, she heard the cannibal coming behind her. Following instructions, she dropped the huckleberries, which instantly became huckleberry bushes. The berries on these bushes looked so good to the cannibal that he stopped to eat some of them.

The girl next dropped the blackberries, causing a blackberry thicket to spring up and delay her pursuer. After the cannibal had passed this obstruction, he found a canebrake on the trail. Here the canes were so thick that he had to carry the chunk stone on his shoulder as he walked along. Last of all, the girl dropped the mud, causing the trail behind her to become very boggy.

Eventually the girl entered a field near her house. "Help me; I am almost caught," she called. Her brothers rushed out to defend her and shot the cannibal with many arrows. But the cannibal did not die because the men did not know the proper way to kill him.

"If you hit him in the ankle, you can kill him," said Red Bird, who was sitting on a limb of a nearby tree. They did as Red Bird suggested and killed the cannibal.

Then the men piled some wood on cannibal's body and set it on fire. After all the wood had been burned, they tossed some of the cannibal's ashes into the air, saying, "You will be blackbirds." The ashes became blackbirds and flew away. The brothers threw more ashes into the air, and these ashes turned into bees when the brothers said, "You will become bees."

In the same manner, they created hornets, which flew away. The next time, wasps appeared, and then yellow jackets followed them. The brothers continued until they had created all sorts of winged insects, including mosquitoes and flies.

Part VI

Ghosts, Witches, and Other Supernatural Beings

A YOUNG HUNTER had looked for game all day long without success. At sunset he realized that he was lost in the dense forest. He built a fire and cooked some meat he carried in a leather pouch. Then the hunter lay down to sleep, weary and completely discouraged.

About the middle of the night he heard someone shouting far away, and he thought, "People are searching for me."

Soon the noise came close, and then it sounded like something howling. Suddenly the frightful howling stopped. A second time the voice sounded afar, drew near, and stopped. Yet a third time the man heard the strange howls. Then the forest became still.

On the second day the hunter resumed his search for the village of his tribe, but could not find it. When night came, he sat down under a tree after he had finished his meal.

Later that night he saw a fire appearing and disappearing in the distance, and he thought, "People are coming to meet me." But it was only a raccoon which drew near, its body giving out a strange light. After scratching up something to eat, it went away.

The young man continued looking for the village on the third day, but he was unsuccessful as before. Again he sat under a tree when night came.

Soon a horned owl-crawfish came from a bright sheet of water in the distance, drew near to the hunter, hooted, and then went away. The owl-crawfish appeared in this manner three times before it finally disappeared.

Although the young hunter was so frightened that he had stayed awake during the past three days, he now became so sleepy that he had to lie down for a while. While he was asleep, he thought he saw someone who was sitting in the top of a tree and who said to him, "Your camp is in the direction in which your head lies."

The hunter was astonished and awoke. He arose and went in the direction in which his head had been pointing. The ghostly advisor was correct, for the young hunter arrived at the village of his tribe before the end of that day.

THE ALABAMAS CAPTURE A WITCH

IN the days of the old men, the Alabamas believed that witches lived
in the community. When a tribesman died as a result of some disease
with which the Alabamas were not familiar, the relatives of the dead
person usually attributed the death to the activity of a witch. No one
could identify the witch, but the Alabamas believed that she could
make amends for her evil deed by washing herself with earth from the
grave of the victim.

One year an epidemic took the lives of several members of the tribe.
The tribal leaders tried everything they knew to stop the epidemic.
When all their efforts failed, the people concluded that the deaths were
the work of a witch.

The chief asked several of the leading men to attend a secret council.
When the Alabamas assembled, the chief said, "I have a plan to capture
the witch. Let us hide near the graveyard after the next burial. When
the witch comes to get earth from the new grave, she will leave a footprint outside the graveyard. Since we know the footprints of all who
live in this village, we will identify the witch by her footprint. Then we
will run to the witch's house and catch her washing herself with earth
from the grave."

The Alabamas agreed that this was a good plan, and they decided to
try it. They also selected a place near the graveyard where they could
hide.

A few days after this secret meeting, another tribesman died. Grief-
stricken relatives and friends gathered outside the log fence around the
graveyard to watch his burial. Sorrowful relatives lingered near the
graveyard long after the burial.

After sunset the chief and his selected group quietly assembled near
the burial ground and hid among the trees. Slowly the hours passed.
Only the hooting of an owl broke the monotony of the Alabamas' long
vigil.

About the middle of the night, the sentinels saw a woman stealthily
approaching the burial ground. The men could not identify the woman
because she wore a blanket around her head and shoulders.

The woman climbed the log fence and walked slowly toward the
new grave. She tarried only long enough to fill a small bag with earth
from the grave. Then she started back to the fence. The concealed

Alabamas noticed that the woman seemed to be walking with the aid of a tree branch.

After the woman disappeared into the forest, the chief and his men discovered that the woman had used the tree branch to rub out her footprints as she walked to the fence. Outside the graveyard her footprints mingled with those of the Alabamas who had attended the burial of their relative and friend.

Two weeks later another person died in the village of the Alabamas. This time the chief added a new feature to his plan for capturing the witch. Under cover of darkness, he and his group used tree branches to obliterate all the footprints around the graveyard. They left a smooth strip of sand around the burial ground.

Again the men kept watch. Again they saw a woman visit the graveyard and approach the newly-made grave. There she filled a bag with earth. Then she blotted out her footprints inside the cemetery and ran into the forest.

Triumphantly the group approached the sand, in which they found a footprint. Scrutiny revealed that the footprint was that of a certain old woman living a short distance away. Quietly and quickly the men ran through the forest to the witch's house, which, to their disappointment, they found to be vacant. But the men located the woman behind her house, busily engaged in scrubbing herself with earth! Without a moment's hesitation the men fiercely closed in upon the witch and killed her with their knives. After completing their grim work, the Alabamas again slipped quietly into the forest.

HOW A HUNTER KILLED A GHOST

A YOUNG MAN followed a big river northward from his village one day and camped in a great forest. He gathered bark to build a shelter, and at sunset he started a fire. About the middle of the night, he heard someone shouting, but he saw no one.

On the second day, he killed a deer, which he brought back to his camp. By the time he had roasted the meat, the sun had gone down and darkness covered the forest.

Soon after he sat down to eat, the hunter heard someone's footsteps.

Presently a ghost came and sat down on the other side of the fire. "Eat meat with me," the hunter invited.

So the ghost ate some of the meat. When the ghost finished, the hunter gave him some more meat. The ghost carried it off with him, and in a little while he came back. The hunter gave the ghost some more venison, which he also took away. As before, he soon came back for more meat.

This continued until the venison was depleted. Then the ghost took the deer skin, and when he had just started off with it, the hunter ran toward the river. He heard the ghost shouting behind him, so he dived into the river and swam a long time beneath the surface before coming up. When he looked back, the hunter saw the ghost standing near the edge of the water. Soon the sun rose, and the ghost was forced to abandon his search and return to his hiding place in a hollow tree.

When the sun was directly overhead, the hunter traveled in the direction from which the ghost had come. As he hunted about, he saw some spunk stuck in the crack of a tree. He pulled the spunk out and saw his venison scattered about inside the tree. Then he put dry deadwood into the hollow tree and set it on fire. The ghost who was hidden inside the tree cried out, but his shouting soon ceased. After making sure the fire had killed the ghost, the hunter returned to his village.

Part VII

Animal and Bird Husbands

THE FLIGHT TO THE TREE

THE FLIGHT TO THE TREE

AN old woman and her granddaughter lived in the forest a short distance from the rest of the tribe. One day the grandmother said she needed some water, so the young girl took a clay bucket and set out for a creek near the cabin.

After she had drawn water, she stood by the edge of the creek for a while. Presently an old buffalo walked to the other side of the creek and called to the girl. After talking a short time, the two went away together.

Since the young girl did not return to her home, the grandmother went into the village to seek help in finding her. None of the villagers had seen the girl. They said they did not know where to start looking.

Finally, an orphan said, "I will try to find her."

"All right. Go into the forest and look for the girl," said the chief of the village. "If you find her, you shall have her as your wife."

The orphan prepared for the search by placing in his shoulder pouch three hen's eggs, a sabia, and three arrows. Two of the arrows were red, and the other was yellow. Then the young man went into the woods to look for the girl.

Soon he saw many buffalo walking around in the forest. The girl he was seeking sat on the ground in the midst of the big animals. By singing a magic song, the orphan caused the buffalo to sleep. Then he seized the girl, who did not want to leave, and carried her toward a bent-over pine tree.

While the two were proceeding toward the tree, first the old buffalo and then all of the others awoke and ran after them. The orphan reached the tree with the girl, climbed it, and sat near the girl on a big limb.

All the buffalo gathered around the tree and nearly made it fall by rubbing against it. But the young man dropped a hen's egg upon the ground, and the tree stood up just as before.

Again the buffalo rubbed against the tree and nearly made it fall. The orphan dropped another hen's egg, which caused the tree to straighten for the second time.

After the young man dropped the third egg in this manner, he shot an arrow through a buffalo. The arrow immediately returned to him. He shot it through another and another of the big animals. The arrow continued to return to the orphan until he had killed all except the old buffalo.

The big animal stamped hard upon the ground, causing pine knots to fly against the tree. But the man caught them and threw them back.

The old buffalo continued to stamp on the ground. Finally, the orphan killed the buffalo by shooting the yellow arrow through him.

Now, the big creature was the girl's husband, so she started crying and told the man that she would not go home. For that he killed her and took her clothes to the village. When he arrived, the people of the village gave a basket of gifts to the orphan for finding the girl.

A TRIP TO THE BEAD-SPITTER

ONE DAY two girls started out to get some beads from Bead-Spitter. By and by they came to a pond. Here they saw Owl, who said that he was searching in the water for a sabia he had lost.

"Where are you going?" asked Owl.

One of the girls replied, "We are going to the home of Bead-Spitter. Which is the trail to his house?"

As Owl pointed with a small stick, he said, "Go along that trail."

Now the deceitful Owl had really indicated the trail which led to his house. He flew through the woods to his house, broke a necklace of beads that was around his sister's neck, and threw the beads to the ground. Then he picked up some of the beads, put them into his mouth, and sat down.

As soon as the two girls arrived, Owl pretended to cough and thereby started spitting out many beads. The two girls concluded that Owl was the Bead-Spitter for whom they had been looking.

That night Owl went to a neighbor's house to dance, and the girls followed later to watch the dancers. Here they saw many beads of all colors scattered around in the house. The two girls became suspicious and started asking questions. They discovered that Owl had deceived them and that they were at last in the home of the real Bead-Spitter. The two girls stayed in Bead-Spitter's house that night.

After all the dancers had left and everything became very quiet, Owl slipped into the house and killed Bead-Spitter with a knife. On the following morning, news of the murder spread among the people in the village, but no one seemed to know who had killed Bead-Spitter.

Since this man had been a person of great importance in the tribe, everybody attended his funeral. Later, the men decided that the one who cut off his own hair and completely filled a basket with it should have the two girls who had been visiting Bead-Spitter. Accordingly, Owl cut off all his sister's hair, but could not fill the basket. The brother of the two girls did fill the basket with his hair, but they did not let him have his sisters.

Then someone suggested, "Let us see who will be the first to kill a white deer. The first to kill one shall have the two girls."

Owl killed a white dog and cut off its head and feet, but the villagers discovered his trick. Although the brother of the two girls killed a white deer, the others insisted upon another test.

This time they decided to hunt for a white turkey. The men got into a large canoe and paddled across the ocean. They agreed to hunt separately, all of them returning to the canoe seven days later. So the men scattered and began hunting.

By and by, the girls' brother killed a white turkey. But when he returned to the place where the hunting party had landed, he found that the others already had started to paddle away. The young man shot arrows into the canoe, and all the hunters except Owl were drowned when the canoe sank. Owl managed to get back to the village by holding onto some pieces of wreckage. Later he took the two girls for his wives.

Meanwhile, the brother of the two girls walked up and down the edge of the ocean trying to find some means of crossing the water. One day Red Bird said to him, "I came to let you know that something big is following you. Make three chunk stones, climb into a willow tree, and sit down." The man believed Red Bird was his friend, so he made three chunk stones and climbed into a willow tree near the ocean.

Presently a cannibal and three spotted panthers came along on the man's trail. When the panthers started to climb the willow tree, the young man threw a chunk stone into the water. Instantly the panthers jumped into the ocean to investigate, but later they returned to the base of the willow tree. Again he threw a chunk stone into the water, and again the panthers jumped in and hunted for the stone. He threw the third stone down, and it also attracted the panthers' attention away from his hiding place.

Finally, the cannibal got so hungry that he couldn't wait any longer for the panthers to catch the man, so he put the panthers into a pot of boiling water. When the panthers had been boiled thoroughly, he took the pot off the fire and ate the animals. Afterward he threw the panther bones into the ocean, and the panthers came to life again when the cannibal called them.

Not until the cannibal and his spotted panthers had gone back into the woods did the young man dare to climb down the willow tree and continue his journey along the edge of the ocean. During his travels he met a hunter, who invited the young traveler to stay in his house for a while.

On the first night, the young man asked Rattlesnake to stay near him as a guard. During the night an old, insane woman tried to kill the sleeping man, but Rattlesnake started rattling, and the woman went away.

The next night White Crane was stationed nearby. White Crane awakened the young man by calling loudly when the old woman came close.

On the third night, a big earthen pot acted as a guard. Again the old woman quietly approached the youth. She tried to hit him with a club, but she only hit the clay pot.

So dangerous had the old woman become that the young man decided he should leave. On the following morning, he killed and roasted forty quail to prepare for his journey.

Then he went to the edge of the ocean where he called out, "My friend," and Alligator came out of the water.

"You are not the one," said the youth, and Alligator began crying and dived out of sight. His second call brought out Turtle, who went sorrowfully back into the ocean when he found that he wasn't wanted.

When the man called the third time, Snake-Crawfish (Horned Snake) came out. "You are the one; come here," commanded the youth.

Then he jumped on Horned Snake's back and tied the roasted quail to the horns. Next, he threw one of the quail into the ocean, and Horned Snake swam after it. When Horned Snake had almost swallowed the meat, the man threw another quail far out in front, and Horned Snake swam toward it.

The traveler continued until all the quail had been eaten. After that, he shot arrows which Horned Snake pursued in the same manner, thinking the arrows were roasted quail. To get the third arrow Horned Snake swam near the shore, whereupon his passenger jumped off.

As the young man climbed the bank, the sand caved in and carried him down. He tried again and eventually reached firm ground. After a short walk through the woods, he hid near Owl's house to see what was happening. In front of the house, he saw his two sisters pounding corn, while Owl sat nearby, making an axe handle.

When the young man finished his inspection, he slipped away to the path leading to the spring. He stuck an arrow in the path and then hid among some trees. Soon his sisters came down the path to get some water from the spring.

"This looks like our brother's arrow," said one of them, as she pointed to an arrow in the trail. In a little while, the young man came out of the woods and greeted his sisters.

"Whose children are these?" he asked, indicating two infants which they were carrying.

"Owl's children," they answered.

Now, the man had formed a plan to get rid of Owl, and to his sisters he gave these instructions: "Take water and fill a kettle. Kindle a fire beneath and make the water boil. Then pick up the children and call Owl. When Owl looks in that direction, put the children into the boiling water and run toward me."

The sisters carefully attended to each detail mentioned by their brother. As they ran down the trail, Owl started after them. When they reached the woods, their brother killed Owl by shooting an arrow through him. Thus, the youth freed his sisters, and all three went back to their village.

Part VIII

Encounters with Monsters

HOW THE ALABAMAS KILLED A MONSTER LIZARD

WHILE the Alabamas still lived in an old town on the Alabama River, the chief of this village assigned six young men to kill bears for the villagers.

Before leaving the town on a hunting trip one day, the six men steamed themselves in the sweat lodge and plunged into a cold creek. Then they went into a dense forest to look for bears.

As they moved through the woods, the six Alabamas inspected the trees carefully. On the third day, they found a tree that looked like a "bear tree"—a hollow tree with scratched bark.

One of the young men climbed a tree growing near the bear tree. He tied dry grass to an arrow, set it on fire, and shot the arrow into a large hole near the top of the bear tree.

Soon the hunters could hear a rumbling which sounded like a bear's angry roar, and which grew louder and louder. From the hole in the hollow tree appeared not a bear, but a horrible-looking monster lizard!

The men on the ground became frightened and ran away in different directions. Their comrade in the tree hid himself among the branches, and from this position he could see the monster lizard running around the tree, looking for the trails of the hunters.

The great lizard found the trail of one of the hunters and rushed toward him. As soon as the monster started on the hunter's trail, the hunter became paralyzed and could not move. The big lizard killed him and placed the body in his hollow tree.

The first hunter had run only a short distance before the monster started on his trail, and the big creature returned with him quickly. The second hunter managed to run much farther, so the monster stayed away longer before returning to his tree.

Soon the monster had brought in four of the hunters. The fifth man, of course, had gone farther than any of the others. Knowing the monster would be on the trail of this man for a considerable length of time, the hunter who had climbed the tree jumped down and ran toward his village.

He had run a long time through the woods before the monster started on his trail. As it happened to others, so now it happened to him: he became paralyzed and fell into a creek. The current carried him to some driftwood caught in a bend of the creek, where he became lodged between two logs so that he could not be seen above the water.

When the monster reached the creek, he roared three times, jumped into the creek, and swam to the pile of driftwood. He hunted all over the top of the driftwood but did not go under the water. Finally, the big lizard left without finding the man.

After the monster left, the hunter was released from his paralysis. He rushed to the village to tell what had happened.

The next day the hunter led the other men of the village to the monster's hollow tree. He climbed the same tree he had climbed before and set the hollow tree on fire with flaming arrows.

While the hunter shot arrows into the hollow tree, the other men carried water and made a boggy place around the base of the hollow tree. When the monster jumped down from his tree, he bogged down in the wet soil. Then the men built a fire around the big lizard and burned him to death.

THE BLACK PANTHER'S REQUEST

NEAR the end of winter, before the grass began to grow, a man went out from his village to hunt bears. He took along a large pack of dogs to trail the bears. The hunter had trained these dogs to bark loudly when they brought a bear to bay. The man then would run to the scene and kill the bear.

One day the dogs began barking near a large pile of rocks. The hunter assumed that the dogs had found a bear, so he started toward the noise. As he approached the rocks, however, he saw a monster lizard dart out from the rocks, seize a dog, and carry it back. Becoming frightened, the hunter turned and ran toward his camp.

After the hunter had covered about half the distance, he stopped and listened. It sounded as if only a few dogs were barking. The next time he stopped he heard nothing. Farther along the trail, he looked back and saw the monster lizard running after him.

The hunter realized that the big lizard was certain to catch him, so he dropped to the ground and lay flat upon his chest. The lizard picked him up with his mouth and started back to his den among the rocks.

Along the trail, the lizard heard something making a scratching noise in a tree nearby. The lizard threw the hunter down, and the man lay still as if dead.

A large, black panther was making the noise, and now the great cat jumped from the tree onto the lizard. The monster tried to seize the panther, but the black animal sprang out of reach. Then it leaped again upon the lizard and sprang into another tree. Each time the panther leaped upon the lizard, he bit the monster deeply. Soon the lizard was seriously wounded and ran away with the panther in pursuit.

The hunter did not move, since he thought the panther might eat him when it returned. He did not know it had come back until it was close by and he heard Black Panther say, "Are you dead?"

At first he did not reply, but soon Black Panther said, "I am here. Do not be afraid, for I will help you."

The hunter then said, "No, I am not dead or even hurt much."

"Can you stand on your feet?" asked Black Panther.

"No," the hunter answered.

"Then climb upon my back, and I will carry you to your village," said Black Panther.

On the way to the village they came upon the bow and arrows the hunter had dropped when the monster lizard was chasing him. Black Panther told him to pick them up and carry them with him. After they reached a point near the hunter's village, Black Panther set the man upon the ground and told him to go the remainder of the distance himself.

The hunter invited Black Panther to come into the village and get all the food he wanted. The panther refused the man's offer, but before departing, he said, "My friend, I have two nephews that I hope you will never harm. One is called Wildcat and the other is House Cat."

The hunter agreed, and all the other people in the village also said they would honor Black Panther's request. They have done so since that day.

THE MONSTER DEER

WHEN Aba Mikko created the creatures of the world, he made only one little fawn. He gave the fawn a special home in the forest and appointed Wildcat to be its guardian. Wildcat, however, killed it.

After Aba Mikko restored the fawn to life, he sent Panther to watch the fawn. Panther, also, proved to be a traitorous murderer, and next Aba Mikko ordered Bird-That-Sits-On-Deer to watch the revived fawn.

Under the care of this bird, the fawn grew and soon became a huge buck—larger than a buffalo. The bird sat on the buck's horn and ate ticks. One day the wind blew from the north, and the little bird flew away to seek shelter in the moss. Next morning, the deer had disappeared and could not be found anywhere.

The people of a certain village wanted to find out where the deer had gone, so they assembled all of the medicine men. These men formed a large circle, in the center of which they built a fire. Next, they made all sorts of medicines to discover where the big buck had gone. One medicine man sat down but could not learn anything. Another sat down to locate the deer, but in vain. Still another sat down and could discover nothing.

Last of all they asked Flying Squirrel to help. He flew up toward the east and remained poised. He stayed up awhile and then came back to the ground. He flew up to the west, remained for some time, and came down. He flew up to the north, stayed aloft a short while, and came down. He flew to the south but quickly returned. Then he said, "The big buck is standing in a small lake south of here."

The medicine men immediately began mixing medicines to summon the deer. Soon the people heard it approaching, but when they saw the buck they became afraid. The deer had grown so large that the villagers believed the awesome creature would kill them. So the men got their bows and arrows and stood ready to shoot it, with ghosts just behind them, panthers in the third row, wolves in the fourth, and wildcats in the fifth. The wildcats, however, became frightened and ran away.

When the huge buck arrived, the men tried to shoot it but failed. The ghosts hit it and the panthers jumped upon it and threw it down. With the help of the wolves, the ghosts and panthers soon killed the monster deer. Then the wildcats came running back and bit it in the throat until they were driven away. While the men were beating the big deer to pieces with sticks, each hair that came loose from the carcass turned into a deer and ran off into the woods. Since that time deer have been plentiful in the land of the Alabamas and Coushattas.

Part IX

Hero Stories

THE MAN WITH HORNS

SOME of the oldest men told about wars between Alabamas and Choctaws. They said that one year, about the end of winter, the Alabamas heard voices of invisible spirits in the air, warning them of wars and misfortunes the future held in store for them.

Not long afterward the Choctaws came from their country west of the Tombigbee River. They began killing Alabamas and destroying some of the lower villages along the Alabama River.

The people of one of the upper villages left their homes and ran into a dense forest to hide. One day they camped among some trees near a beautiful stream. Since the camp seemed to be in a safe place, with an abundance of food, the Alabamas decided to remain there several days.

Early the next morning, a woman went to the creek for her daily bath. She plunged into the water four times. When she emerged from the water the fourth time, she saw a baby in a large clay bowl near the edge of the stream. She was afraid to pick up the baby, since the Choctaws might have used the child to set a trap. The woman hurried to the Alabama camp to report what she had seen.

On the chief's orders some of the men brought the baby to the camp. It was a very beautiful male child. The chief said that he thought this was an unusual child and would bring luck to the tribe.

By the next morning the child had grown to the size of an eight-year-old boy. The people marveled. Everyone was convinced now that the boy was not just an ordinary person.

The next day, he had grown to the size of a sixteen-year-old boy. On the third day, he was fully grown and had large horns sticking out from his head. Since the stranger had no clothes large enough to fit him, the chief ordered the men of the camp to bring clothes to "Horned Man," as he was called by the Alabamas.

Horned Man told the people that he had come to help them, but that they also would have to help themselves. Then he called for the bravest men in the camp.

"Bring to me the head of the largest wolf you can find," he said to the warriors.

Three days later the hunting party returned with the head of a large wolf. Horned Man put the wolf's head on top of a pole in the center of the camp ground.

Immediately the head began turning around and around. It looked in all directions. Finally it stopped and pointed to the east.

"The wolf's head indicates that Choctaws are approaching from the east," said Horned Man. Then he led the Alabamas to a hiding place to the south.

The next day the wolf's head pointed to the west. This time Horned Man led the Alabamas to a thicket in the north.

"The wolf's head will always point to your enemies," said Horned Man. "But if the head should stop pointing and fall to the ground, this will indicate that you are surrounded by enemies."

By watching the wolf's head closely, the Alabamas managed to slip away from the Choctaws for a long time. But one day the head became uncertain in its movements. It turned slowly without pointing very long in any one direction. Suddenly it fell to the ground.

At this signal the Alabamas grasped their axes and positioned themselves for battle. The enemy warriors rushed into camp, and the fighting began. Many of the enemy tribesmen were killed, while the Alabamas did not lose a man.

"Bring Horned Man to me," said the chief, "so I can thank him for helping us win this victory."

They looked all over the woods but could not find Horned Man. He had disappeared. And none of the Alabamas ever saw him again.

LODGE BOY AND LOST BOY

IN the old days, a hunter and his son lived in a cabin near a large river. The father spent most of his time in the forest hunting bear, deer, and other animals. His son, who was called "Lodge Boy," cleaned the cabin, cooked meals, and cultivated vegetables. Lodge Boy amused himself by shooting arrows at various types of targets.

One day Lodge Boy said to his father, "Make some arrows for me."

Several days later the boy repeated the request for more arrows. "How does it happen," asked his father, "that you use so many arrows? Where are the others I made for you?"

"A boy comes here while you are away," answered Lodge Boy, "and we have shooting contests. We bet arrows, and he won all of them."

"When he comes back, you must catch him," said the father.

He made more arrows for his son, and the next day he hid near the cabin to watch. The strange boy came to the cabin again, and Lodge Boy seized him. While the boys wrestled, the hunter tied the second boy with deerskin strips.

After three days the wild boy quieted down when he realized the hunter and his son were friends and wanted him to live with them. The hunter untied the strange youth and gave him a name which means "Lost Boy."

One night, while the three sat near a fire in the cabin talking about a recent hunting trip, they heard someone yelling on the opposite side of the river. When they went to the river's edge, they saw a crippled man on the opposite side. He said he wanted to cross the river.

Lost Boy started to take the man across in a canoe, but the hunter warned him not to help the stranger. He said that the opposite side of the river was the home of the evil spirits who sometimes disguised themselves in order to get into the land of the Alabamas and Coushattas.

About the end of winter, the hunter made preparations for a trip to a distant village to exchange his pelts for food and clothing. Before leaving, he warned the boys again that they should not go across the river. Then he picked up his pack and walked away into the forest.

The two boys didn't have much to do. After they cleaned the cabin each day, they spent the remainder of the time practicing with bows and arrows.

One day they heard horrible screams coming from the other side of the river. The boys thought that someone must be injured and in need of help. In their excitement they forgot the warning of the hunter. They jumped into a canoe and rowed across the river.

Beneath a tree on the bank, the boys saw an old man, swaying from side to side and groaning. When the boys approached, the old man explained that he could not walk but had to depend on others to carry him from place to place. He begged the boys to take him in their canoe.

The old man seemed to be a harmless cripple, so Lost Boy carried him to the canoe. Then Old Man said he could not sit alone and must sit on Lost Boy's back. In this manner the boys carried him across the river.

He next asked Lost Boy to carry him to the hunter's house. When Lost Boy picked him up, Old Man laughed and locked his arms around Lost Boy, who now realized that Old Man intended to hurt him. Lost

Boy rolled on the ground trying to get rid of Old Man, but he could not dislodge the cripple.

A few days later the hunter came back. Lost Boy still could not get rid of Old Man, so the hunter told his son to heat some water. When the water started boiling, the hunter poured it on Old Man, who ran screaming under the house. There, to this day, his spirit hides and will jump on anybody who isn't watching.

THE DIRTY BOY

NEAR an Alabama village, long ago, lived a boy whose father and mother died when he was very young. An old woman who had known his parents took care of the boy and raised him as her son. She gave him a name which means "Orphan." The woman wanted to keep the boy with her, and she told him not to go into the nearby valley where the village was located.

One time Orphan went into a canebrake and saw a strange animal. He came back and asked the old woman about it.

"That thing is a bear," she said.

On another occasion he asked her, "What thing looks like a big bird and always walks around?"

She answered, "That is a turkey."

Later, Orphan went hunting, found some turkeys, and chased them to the edge of a cliff. They kept going until they entered the village in the valley. The boy stood there looking at the village a while. Then he returned to his foster mother and told her what he had seen.

The old woman realized to her sorrow that the time had come for Orphan to leave her and live among the people in the village. "Go into the forest and kill some redbirds and bluejays," she said.

Since the boy was an expert marksman with bow and arrow, it didn't take him long to kill a large number of birds. The old woman picked out the feathers and made a beautiful headdress for him. Next, she gave him a flute she had made.

"Put on your headdress and go into the village, blowing your flute," she directed, so Orphan started out with them.

When he came within sight of the village, he blew the flute, and many redbirds and bluejays began singing. While he was going along blowing his flute, he met Rabbit, who was carrying some deerskin cords.

"I am going to tie up the legs of turtles and take them out of the water. This is a lot of fun; go with me," said Rabbit. He urged Orphan so strongly to accompany him that the young man finally agreed to go. When they came to the water, they pulled off their clothes and laid them on the ground.

"When I say 'Now,' we will dive," said Rabbit, and on this signal they dived. Rabbit went down, but came right up. While his companion was still under the water, Rabbit ran off with Orphan's headdress and flute.

Orphan stayed in the water until he had tied up many turtles and brought them out. When he found that Rabbit had carried off the headdress and flute, he decided to make the best of the situation somehow. So he picked up the turtles and started off.

On the way he came to a persimmon tree, shook it, and ate some of the fruit. He mashed a few of the persimmons in his hands and rubbed them all over his shirt. Then he took the turtles and went on.

When he reached the village, nearly everybody was unfriendly to the dirty young man. Orphan stopped at a certain house and remained standing outside. Presently a girl came out and looked at him. Then she went inside and said to her mother, "There is a young man standing out there."

"Bring him here," said the mother, so the young girl told Orphan to come into the house. He gave the turtles to the girl's mother, who prepared them for supper.

It happened that Orphan and the girl married, and one day the young man and his wife went to a big creek to bathe. As soon as they arrived there, the man dived out of sight under the water and came out on the other side of the creek. He dived again and came out near his wife. After he had dived back and forth under the water three times, both returned to the village.

"Tell all of your people to look at the place in the creek where I dived," he said to his wife. So his wife told all of her people. The villagers did as the young man instructed, and they found the water was white with many fish, which they gathered in baskets and later ate.

Rabbit heard stories of Orphan's accomplishment and tried to imitate him. Rabbit took his wife to the creek, dived back and forth three times, and told his wife to tell her relatives to go to the creek and look. All went down, but there was nothing there except a single minnow floating upon the surface.

Afterward Orphan went hunting and traveled along near the creek. Presently he killed a deer and hung its body upon a tree. Then he killed several more deer, each of which he treated in the same manner as the first. When he returned home, he said to his wife, "Tell your people to follow around where I have been hunting."

Accordingly, the village residents took three horses and set out. They found dead deer hanging on many trees along the trail. The people gathered the deer and brought them home on the horses' backs. They cooked the deer and had enough venison to last for many days.

Then Rabbit also went hunting. When he came to the place where Orphan killed his first deer, Rabbit found the liver which the man had thrown away, cut it into small pieces, and hung them up. At each place where Orphan had killed a deer, Rabbit hung pieces of liver.

He later said to his wife, "Let your people hunt where I have been." They did so, but found only small pieces of liver to bring home.

Next Orphan combed his wife's hair and parted it. Then he split her in two with a club so cleverly that now he had two wives instead of one.

Rabbit heard of it and thought, "I will do the same thing. I will tell my wife to sit with her hair combed, and then I will hit her with a club in the same manner." But when Rabbit tried it, his wife fell down dead.

Consequently, some men with dogs set out after Rabbit, who had to flee through the forest. After Rabbit had run for a long time, he took refuge in a hollow tree.

The men stationed White Crane in front of the tree to watch Rabbit while they went for an axe. They gave Crane a deerskin cord with which to tie Rabbit in case he tried to escape.

After the men were out of sight, Rabbit asked Crane to look inside. Crane did so, and Rabbit grabbed the leather cord. Then he tied it around Crane's neck and fastened him to the tree. Next, Rabbit picked up a big switch and beat Crane until the bird turned blue. Since that day people called this bird Blue Crane.

When the people allowed Rabbit to return to the village, he heard that Orphan had changed a small hut into a beautiful house. Rabbit asked Orphan how he managed to do this. Orphan decided to play a trick on Rabbit, so he said that he chopped some square blocks, placed them in the shape of a house, and then kicked the house.

Since it seemed so easy to build a pretty house in this manner, Rabbit resolved to build one for himself. He chopped the blocks, placed them in the shape of a house, and then kicked the house. The blocks fell down on Rabbit and crushed him to death.

THE PIGEON HAWK'S GIFT

A HUNTER had been tramping through the woods all day long without finding any deer. He needed a change of luck, so he opened the buckskin pouch containing his magic sabia, took out a little red paint, and put it on his cheeks. But this time the charm did not help him. He still did not see any game.

When the sun went down, he built a fire in a hollow stump and put some tobacco under the fire to keep away evil spirits. Next, he sat down on a log, ate a few mouthfuls of parched ground corn, and began repairing his moccasins.

While he was sitting there, Pigeon Hawk flew down and perched on his knee. Soon Owl, who had been trying to catch Pigeon Hawk, swooped down and stood on the opposite side of the campfire.

"Throw Pigeon Hawk over to me. I want to kill him," said Owl.

But Pigeon Hawk said, "No, don't throw me over there."

"Throw him over to me," said Owl, "and I will enable you to see at night."

Then Pigeon Hawk said, "This Owl has an evil spirit. Don't throw me over to him, and when day comes I will give you good hunting."

Accordingly, the hunter protected Pigeon Hawk throughout the night. When day began to break, Owl hooted and flew up to the top of a tree, where he sat half blinded by the sun.

Since Owl now could not see very well, Pigeon Hawk quietly flew up behind Owl and cut off his head. Then Pigeon Hawk flew back to the camp, pulled out a short wing feather, and gave it to his friend.

"Keep this and you can kill anything," said Pigeon Hawk.

After that the man became a good hunter. He killed bear, deer, turkey, and other kinds of game on his hunting trips.

Part X

Historical Sketches

AN Alabama warrior with a roving disposition crossed the Tombigbee River one day, and the Choctaws captured him. This young man lived with the Choctaws and later fought with his captors against the Alabamas.

On one occasion, the Choctaws and Alabamas fought all day, and at night the Alabamas camped near a creek surrounded by high bluffs. The Choctaws built fires on the edges of the bluffs and kept a ring of guards around their enemies.

The Alabama who had been captured by the Choctaws rolled rocks down upon the Alabamas camped along the creek. But the Choctaws still did not trust the renegade Alabama. Later that night they put him in a hollow tree so he would not be near when the fighting resumed the next day.

During the night, the trapped Alabamas called upon one of their warriors to make it rain. The man selected for this task began chanting and shaking a gourd rattle until the skies became cloudy and rain fell. It rained continuously until the water put out all of the Choctaw fires on the bluffs surrounding the Alabamas.

Then one of the Alabama warriors crawled between the Choctaw watchmen. He walked around howling like a fox and then made his way back to the Alabama campsite. There he assured the Alabamas that they could escape through the Choctaw line, and all of them crawled past their enemies.

After the Alabamas escaped, they went to the place where the renegade Alabama was stationed in a hollow tree. They called out in the Choctaw language, and the Alabama came down from the tree.

Then the warriors killed the renegade and cut off his head. They put the head on a stick near the Alabama villages as a warning to anyone else who might consider helping the Choctaws in the future.

THE ALABAMAS TRAVEL WESTWARD

DURING the early years the Alabamas ate acorns and cane sprouts. Later they made bows and arrows to kill deer. To kindle a fire, they used as a drill the stem of a weed called hassala'po (plant-with-which-to-make-fire), which is like sassafras, and the wood of a tree called baksa (bass) for a base stick.

They built their village near a large river and stayed there a long time. Presently they came in contact with the Choctaws and warred against them, almost destroying one Choctaw town. So the Choctaws became disheartened and wanted to make peace.

For this purpose the Choctaws selected a poor man, to whom they promised to give two girls if he were successful in his peace mission. Then they gave him a white deerskin shirt, deerskin leggings, and moccasins. Next they put several strings of white beads about his neck and a rattle in his hand.

Thus equipped, the Choctaw peace emissary crossed to the first Alabama village, shaking his rattle and singing as he went. When the Alabamas heard him they came out, took hold of him, and accompanied him to the village. When they came near the town, they raised the Choctaw on their backs and entered the place in this manner, singing continuously.

When they set him down, he talked to them for a long time, laying down one string of white beads as he did so. Then he set out for another Alabama village, accompanied as before.

At the second village, he made another long talk and laid out a second string of white beads. He did the same at the third village. This was the end of his peace mission, and he returned to the Choctaws who gave him the girls as they had promised.

One summer an Alabama said he wanted to go west, and several wished to go with him. But a berdache (half-man) tried to stop him. "Why are you going?" he asked.

To this question the Alabama replied, "I am going in order to kill turkey, deer, and other animals; after that I will return."

"There are plenty of turkey and deer here," said the berdache.

But the Alabama still wanted to go, and after they had argued for some time the berdache said, "You are a man, but you want to run away. I will not run away. I will not run, although my grandfather used to say that the English are all hard fighters. When they come, I will take a knife, lie down under the bed, and keep striking at them until they kill me."

Nevertheless, the Alabama and his friends started off. They came to a river, made canoes, and proceeded along it a great distance until they finally reached a Choctaw settlement. They stopped for a while, thinking that these people were friends. Presently, though, the Alabamas observed that the Choctaws were making arrows. So the Alabamas got into their canoes and continued down the river.

By and by they came upon many bears swimming in the river. Some wanted to kill them, but others cautioned against shooting the animals. Later they heard noises behind them and one of the men said, "People are following us."

A short distance ahead they saw many canes in the mouth of a creek which flowed into the river. They shoved their canoes into this cane-brake and waited. After a while they heard the Choctaw canoes pass, but the Alabamas decided to stay in the canebrake all that night.

Just before the sun came up, they heard the sounds of the Choctaw war-party again. Not until the Choctaws went by and disappeared up the river did the Alabamas dare to continue their journey.

A few days later the travelers arrived at the house of a white man. He exchanged corn for venison and told them that the route by the river they had intended to take was very long and that he knew a shorter way. So he tied oxen to their canoes and dragged them across a narrow neck of land to another river.

Farther down this river they stopped at a trading post belonging to a white blacksmith. From him the Alabamas got knives and axes in exchange for venison.

Some Choctaws living nearby said to them. "There is no war here. There is peace. We are friends of the Alabamas."

Afterward, however, some of both tribes got drunk on whiskey bought at the store and wanted to fight. But the Alabamas who stayed sober took their people down to the canoes, put them in, and started along.

After leaving the blacksmith, the Alabamas went to Bayou Boeuf. Later they moved to Opelousas, Louisiana, and still later they settled Peach-Tree Village in Tyler County, Texas.

There were many Alabamas at that time, and they separated into three villages. Peach-Tree Village was northeast of present Chester,

Texas. Another was a few miles north of Woodville near the Neches River and was called "Cane Island" because many canes were found along a nearby creek. The third village was called Fenced-in Village. They were living in these towns when the war between Texas and Mexico broke out.

General Houston had visited the Alabamas and asked them not to fight with either side during the war. Therefore, the Alabamas remained neutral, and a few went back to Louisiana. To show that they were neutral, the Alabamas who stayed in Peach-Tree Village hung a large piece of white cloth every time a group of fleeing Texans approached the village. Some of the whites who passed through Peach-Tree Village were almost perishing with hunger. The Alabamas gave them food and drink.

After the white people left the region, the Mexicans went to a town on a big river. The soldiers opened the abandoned store and used the goods. Some of the soldiers wanted to cross the big river near the town and threw bales of cotton into the water to form a temporary bridge. The Mexicans crossed the river and drove away some Indians who were camping nearby.

From a distant place some white men came to fight the Mexicans. Several of the whites went around the town and broke down a bridge over a creek so the Mexicans couldn't escape in that direction. Then a big fight started. The soldiers fired many guns.

Of all the Mexicans who took part in the battle, only their General Santa Anna and a few others got away. The general fell down in a thicket. While he was in the thicket, two deer whistled, indicating to the whites where Santa Anna was hiding.

The Texans captured the Mexican general and took him to their camp. After Santa Anna agreed to give up all the land in this country and promised not to bother the white people any more, the Texans allowed him to get into a boat and sail away.

CHIEF COLITA OF THE COUSHATTA INDIANS

IN the year 1834 a number of colonists made their way into that section of Texas now known as Montgomery County. On the morning of

April 18, 1836, a messenger came to the settlements in this region and advised the colonists of the approach of the Mexican Army under Santa Anna. No sooner had the messenger continued his journey through East Texas than refugees from the Brazos River area began to pass in haste to avoid the oncoming devastation.

The waters of the Trinity seemed to offer refuge to the frightened Texans, who felt that it would place a barrier between them and the Napoleon of the West after they had crossed it. Immediately the Montgomery County settlers made ready to join the "Runaway Scrape," and long before nightfall they were traveling eastward along Long King's Trace. Some were in wagons, others on horseback, and many of the less fortunate were forced to travel on foot.

When the refugees reached the Trinity River, they found that the ferry boat had been washed away! The April showers had proved to be torrents, and the usually peaceful stream was a wide and muddy barrier between Texans and the territory they considered a haven.

More threatening than the murky Trinity were some Indians who appeared on the opposite bank. Despair must have rushed with a mighty surge over the weary and wet pioneers as they faced apparent annihilation at the hands of the Indians. Could it be the Kickapoo Tribe on march to join Santa Anna? Was it a band sent by the Mexicans to cut them off before they reached Louisiana?

Every man held his gun cautiously but surely. Through the dim haze which enveloped the river and the misty rain which was falling, the group of Indians could be seen gathered near the ferry landing on the opposite side of the river. The colonists thought that in a few minutes the Indians would attack them. Retreat was impossible.

The heavy, rich black land of the bottoms was a veritable mire. All afternoon they had labored from one bog to another with the wagons, and now they were completely fatigued. Time would not pass. The Indians on the opposite bank seemed as still as the nearby oak and pecan trees.

Suddenly a lone Indian reined his horse down the bank to the water, hesitated, and then plunged in. Would the others follow? Halfway across the muddy, rolling water, the rider held forth his hand and boomed a greeting. It was Colita, chief of the friendly Coushattas. For a swift second the refugees were speechless. Then the woods rang with their shouts of rejoicing.

The refugees advised Colita of their plight and of the approach of the Mexicans. At a signal from their chief, the Coushattas turned their horses into the river and quickly made the other bank. They cut down trees and fastened logs to the sides of the wagons to convert them into improvised rafts. In a few hours the Texans, tired, wet, and famished, had crossed safely to the eastern side of the Trinity.

Coushatta women gathered from the nearby Long King Village. They made fires and put meat into large clay pots to boil. They had an abundance of meat to cook, because General Houston had asked them to be prepared to help the refugees as they fled eastward.

While the hungry whites ate the hasty meal and warmed their hearts in this new-found hospitality, a scream broke from a startled and delirious mother. In the frenzy of guarding her nine children in the hazardous crossing of the river, she had left one of her babies asleep in a dismantled wagon on the other side. Chief Colita caught her almost incoherent words and again forced his horse across the turbulent water. He quickly returned, holding the crying baby above his head, and placed her in her mother's arms.

When the refugees finished the meal, a few of the leaders held council with Colita. Indian country still lay between them and Louisiana, and the colonists had heard rumors that several Indian tribes, influenced by Mexican agents, would pillage the East Texas settlements at any time. But Colita was mindful of these dangers and soon relieved the anxiety of the whites. Keeping his pledge to General Houston to help protect the white people against such raids, Colita dispatched a strong guard of his warriors to accompany the Texans to the Louisiana border.

Four days after the harrowing crossing of the Trinity, the band of refugees, now greatly enlarged by other settlers fleeing from the common danger, was surprised by the approach of a group of men from the rear. It was Colita and a few of his men coming to bring the news of the victory at San Jacinto. In scant English, Colita told the news as it had been given to him by a runner sent by General Houston with the admonition that it be taken as quickly as possible to the settlers who had been forced to leave their homes.

Part XI

Miscellaneous Tales

THE PYGMIES

SOME pygmies and a hunter—a member of the Alabama tribe—were traveling together through the forest to a distant village. On the first day, they went hunting for meat and killed a rabbit. The pygmies wanted to skin it on the spot, but the hunter carried it back to camp. The travelers threw it on the fire, singed it, and cooked it. The pygmies ate a little and stopped, while the man continued eating until it was gone.

On the next day, they chased a bear and killed it. The hunter wanted to skin the bear immediately, but the pygmies grabbed the bear's legs and carried it to the camp. After they had cooked it, the Alabama ate a little and stopped, but the pygmies kept on eating until it was all gone.

On the third day, they resumed their journey and came to a creek which the man jumped across. The pygmies, however, could not cross it. Then the hunter placed a log over the stream to form a foot bridge, and the pygmies walked safely to the opposite side.

Later, the travelers came to a big river which the Alabama could not cross. This time the pygmies solved the problem: they tied some logs together to make a raft which they used to cross the stream.

On the fourth day, the pygmies said that they were going to war. They had bows about ten inches long, cane arrows with rock tips, axes, and blowguns made from hollowed-out cane.

The first enemy they found was a hive of yellow jackets with which they began to fight. The yellow jackets stung some of the pygmies to death, but the hunter killed the yellow jackets by hitting them with a large bush. The pygmies were grateful for this man's help, and these small people and the Alabamas have been friends to this date.

THE MAN WHO BECAME A SNAKE

TWO brothers went hunting together, and just before sunset one day they camped near a big river. While the older brother gathered bark to put up a shelter, the younger one went to catch fish.

The fisherman cut several canes near the water's edge. He split the canes and tied the strips together to form a cage-trap with a funnel-shaped entrance. Then he waded into the river and secured the trap to a tree stump with a long strip of deerskin.

When the fisherman checked his trap after sunset, he found an unusual catfish. This creature was yellow with red and black spots scattered over its body.

The man who had trapped the fish wanted to cook and eat it. But his brother said, "The old people say that a fish colored like this one is not good. Something terrible will happen to you. Throw it in the river."

"I don't believe what the old people say," the other man said. "I am hungry and will eat the fish." So he cooked the catfish and ate it.

Soon afterward night came, and the brothers lay down on opposite sides of the fire. Late that night the older brother awoke to find his companion groaning and rolling around on the ground in agony.

"What is wrong?" he asked.

"I have a strange feeling," replied the other. "Look at me and see what is happening."

The older man lighted a pine knot and examined his brother. He saw that the body of the fish eater was beginning to assume a curious shape. Soon the legs of the unfortunate man began to grow together, and the lower part of his body turned into a snake.

Next, the man's arms sank into his body, and the skin took on a scaly appearance that mounted gradually to the neck. Finally, his head changed into a tie-snake's head. Then the tie-snake crawled away from the fire and plunged into the river, where he has lived since that time.

THE ESCAPE FROM AN EAGLE

WHILE the Alabamas still lived in an old town on the Alabama River, the people of this settlement went out into the mountains one year on a great hunt. One man who had gone ahead to look for a campsite climbed to the top of a high ridge and saw a high mountain on the other side.

He descended from the ridge and began walking around the sides of the high mountain. Suddenly a big eagle flew down, seized him, and carried him to the top of the mountain. The eagle threw the man into a nest to be food for some eaglets, but he escaped and hid in a rocky cave.

From the cave, the man watched the eaglets grow bigger, and soon they were able to fly a short distance. Since the mother eagle always flew away early in the morning and returned late in the afternoon, the man thought, "I will ride one of the eaglets to the ground while the mother eagle is away."

So he cut a big stick to take with him. By and by the old eagle flew away. Quickly the Alabama carried an eaglet to the edge of a cliff, mounted it, and made it start downward by striking it on the head. When the eaglet would try to fly upward, the man would hit it on the head and make it fly downward. In this manner he soon reached level ground again.

ABA MIKKO'S SON AND THE CORN GRINDER

ABA MIKKO, the Great Chief of the earth and sky, was very sad. Some of his people on earth were quarreling. Aba Mikko was puzzled. He called a council of the wisest men and asked for their advice.

The councilors smoked many pipes in silence. Finally, the oldest man said, "Send Aba Mikko's son to earth. He can stop the quarreling among the people."

The others agreed this was a good plan. So Aba Mikko's son picked up a peace pipe and went down to earth.

When he reached a village, he walked among the people and talked to them about treating their neighbors as friends. But some of the inhabitants started plotting against him. They caught him and, although they wanted to kill him, they were afraid to harm him.

It happened that a blind corn-grinder lived in this village. One plotter sent for the old corn-grinder and placed him on a log in the square-ground. Then he placed the point of a spear against the side of Aba Mikko's son, who was tied to a tree. Next he placed the handle of the spear in the hands of the corn-grinder and told him to push. The blind man did so and unwittingly killed Aba Mikko's son, who remained standing, to the amazement of the spectators. Some of the blood of the dead visitor fell on the eyes of the blind corn-grinder, and the old man regained his sight. When the corn-grinder saw that he had killed someone, he died but remained standing.

Then an even greater miracle occurred. There seemed to be two strangers and two corn-grinders. The two newcomers were the spirits of the two dead men. As the people watched spellbound, the spirit of Aba Mikko's son led the spirit of the corn-grinder to a beautiful country far above the earth.

Appendix

THE APPENDIX indicates tale-types and motifs for the myths and folktales presented in this book. (For definitions of "tale-type" and "motif," see Glossary.)

The utility of classifying tales found in folklore has been recognized for nearly three-quarters of a century. A major step toward a classification framework for tale-types was made by Antti Aarne in 1910, and this system was revised and enlarged by Stith Thompson in *The Types of the Folk-Tale.* The drawback of Thompson's publication for Indian folklore, however, stems from its development for analysis of primarily European folklore.

For this Alabama-Coushatta collection, the classification system presented in "The Types of North-American Indian Tales"—a doctoral dissertation by Remedios Wycoco Moore—was used to assign tale-type numbers. The nucleus of this study is Stith Thompson's *Tales of the North-American Indians.* Thompson annotated only the representative tales selected for his book; Moore's study goes further and provides a broader array of North American Indian tale-types for use in classifying the tales of a collection such as the Alabama-Coushatta narratives.

Appropriate numbers were located in Moore's tale-type index for many of the narratives in the present work. For each of the other narratives, either a new number was assigned under an existing category or the plus sign (+) was used when the position of a new entry in the tale-type index could be allocated only to a general classification.

Motifs listed in the appendix were catalogued according to a modification of the system developed by Stith Thompson in *Motif-Index of Folk-Literature.* As far as possible, a corresponding number from Thompson's index is shown for each motif. For many motifs, however, it was necessary to assign new numbers by extrapolation or by using the plus sign (+) to indicate the closest approximation within Thompson's classification framework.

In addition to the list of motifs by story shown in this appendix, another grouping of these motifs has been prepared—a cross-classification of motifs in relation to Thompson's framework, with references to the tales in this collection. This cross-classification may be obtained from the editor of this book.

CREATION OF THE EARTH: Tale-Type Nos. 101, 102, 133; Motifs: primeval water, A810; earth diver, A812.4; origin of the land, A952.1; creation of mountains, A961.1; bird scouts sent out from raft, A1021.2; speaking animals, B211; speaking birds, B211.3; animals and birds in community action, B239.

ORIGIN OF THE ALABAMA AND COUSHATTA TRIBES: Tale-Type Nos. 215, 221, 272; Motifs: emergence from cave, A1232.3; Alabamas and Coushattas made from clay, A1241; language differences, A1333.2; origin of American Indian tribes, A1611.1.3.

ABA MIKKO ARRANGES THE MONTHS AND SEASONS: Tale-Type Nos. 307A, 310+; Motifs: heat causes distress to mankind, A720.2; attributes of the sun, A738; nature and condition of the moon, A759; nature and condition of the earth (flat), A870+; natural order—general, A1119; weather phenomena, A1149; determination of seasons, A1150; determination of months, A1160; why certain animals serve mankind, A2513; speaking animals, B211; speaking birds, B211.3; grateful animals, B350; helpful horse, B401; helpful domestic beasts—misc., B429; helpful wild beasts—misc., B449; helpful birds—general, B469; sacred person, V206.

THE ORIGIN OF CORN AND TOBACCO: Tale-Type Nos. 235B, 254, 291+; Motifs: acquisition of food supply, A1429; plants created by direct divine agency, A2634; origin of plant cultivation, A2800+; tabu: eating certain things, C229; size of object transformed, D489.9; magic pot, D1171.1; helpful supernatural persons disguised as hunters, N810.5+.

HOW THE SUN CAME TO THE SKY: Tale-Type No. 24; Motifs: the sun is kept in a clay pot, A721.0.1; the sun is restored to the sky, A721.3; the sun is caught, A728; animal characteristics as reward, A2229.7; speaking animals, B211; speaking birds, B211.3; animals and birds in community action, B239; helpful wren, B451.3; helpful buzzard, B455.1; theft by hoodwinking the sun's guardian, K341; dupe's property destroyed, K1410+; deeds rewarded, Q99; sun captured, R9.1.

HOW WATER WAS LOST AND RECOVERED: Tale-Type No. 304; Motifs: action of Creator in restoring natural order, A89; worldwide drought, A1009; release of impounded water, A1111+; helpful birds—general, B469; wagers and gambling, N99; sacred person, V206.

HOW FIRE CAME TO THE ALABAMAS AND COUSHATTAS: Tale-Type No. 263; Motifs: four cardinal directions, A1182+; origin of fire, A1414+; speaking animals, B211; inanimate object (pot) acts as if living, F1009.5.

WHY SICKNESS STILL EXISTS ON THE EARTH: Tale-Type No. 299; Motifs: speaking birds, B211.3; beginnings of trouble for man, A1342; government, P599; existence of sickness, U250+.

THE GREAT FLOOD: Tale-Type No. 151; Motifs: deluge, A1019; escape from deluge, A1021; birds cling to sky in flood—cause of feather colors, A2211.7; characteristics obtained during deluge, A2291; speaking animals, B211; animal grateful for relief from pain, B380+.

WHIPPOORWILL: Tale-Type No. 355+; Motifs: four cardinal directions,

A1182+; punishment for theft, A2238+; speaking animals, B211; speaking birds, B211.3; ranking of animals and birds in community, B220+; animals and birds in community action, B239; thief is detected, K420+; government, P599; ranking in society, P600+; misdeeds concerning property—punishment, Q277; humiliating punishment, Q499.

WHY TURTLE'S SHELL IS DIVIDED INTO SQUARES: Tale-Type No. 355+; Motifs: animal characteristics as reward, A2229.7; origin of body covering, A2310+; miscellaneous bodily features, A2380+; markings on turtle's back, A2412.5.1; speaking animals, B211; reward of helpful animal, B329; repair of shell, B390+; helpful ants, B481.1; helpful turtle, B491.5; race won by deception, K11.1; kindness to animals rewarded, Q51.

WHY OPOSSUM'S TAIL IS BARE: Tale-Type No. 355+; Motifs: obtaining another animal's characteristics, A2240+; why opossum has bare tail, A2317.12; appearance of extremities, A2378; animal characteristics: mobility, A2470+; speaking animals, B211; fanciful bodily members of animals, B720+; fanciful habits of animals, B750+; deception through false doctoring, K1019; arrogance repaid, L430+; unfavorable trait of character—pride, vanity, W110+.

THE STORY OF CROW: Tale-Type No. 354+; Motifs: animal from body of slain person, A1724.1; creation of crow, A1919; helpful birds—general, B469; helpful bumblebees, B481.3.1; helpful wasps, B481.4; helpful hornets, B481.5; transformation: man to crow, D151.4; transformation: person to frog, D195; transformation: frog to person, D395; reincarnation as bird, E650+; extraordinary occurrences concerning animals, F989.29; government: council meeting, P599.

A RACE BETWEEN CRANE AND HUMMINGBIRD: Tale-Type No. 354+; Motifs: birds race, winner to have choice of habitat, A2252.1; habitat established by contest (race), A2433.1.1; speaking birds, B211.3; fanciful habits of birds, B750+; decision made by contest, H217; brain vs. brawn, L310+, Z209.1; wagers and gambling, N99; unfavorable trait of character—pride, vanity, W110+.

WHY TURTLE HAS RED EYES: Tale-Type No. 354+; Motifs: animal characteristics as punishment, A2239.11; miscellaneous bodily features, A2380+; speaking animals, B211; reward of helpful animal, B329; helpful turtle, B491.5; deceiver falls into own trap, K1610.

WHY OPOSSUM CARRIES HER CHILDREN IN A POUCH: Tale-Type No. 354+; Motifs: change in ancient animal, A2210+; miscellaneous bodily features, A2380+; speaking animals, B211; helpful animal, B490+; abduction, R10+; places of captivity: hole in rocks, R45.3.

WHY THE CATFISH HAS A FLAT HEAD: Tale-Type No. 354+; Motifs: trampling causes change in head structure, A2213.2; shape of head, A2320+; speaking animals, B211; animal community, B223; parliament of fishes, B233; animal warfare, B260+.

A JOURNEY TO THE SKY: Tale-Type No. 1052; Motifs: nature and condition of the sun, A720+; nature and condition of the earth, A870+; origin cultivation of new plants, A1425; origin of various plant forms, A2630+; mythical beasts and hybrids, B19.9; horned snake, B91.3; helpful mythical animal, B498; mythical animal carries men, B551; giant sea monster, B877.1; touching things in other world, C500+; transformation: one animal to another, D410+; transformation: object to animal (mountain to tortoise), D440+; land of the dead, E481; animal ghosts, E522; ghosts of objects, E530+; perils of the soul, E750+; ascent to the sky, F10+; access to other world, F50+; nature of the other world: joy, F165.6; nature of the other world: animals in harmony, F167.1; nature of the other world: peace, F173.2; spirits (general), F419; rising and falling sky, F791; extraordinary nature phenomena, F960+; extraordinary occurrences concerning animals, F989.29; quest voluntarily undertaken, H1220+; quest to the other world, H1260; deceptive bargain—bargain implicit, K250+; helpful water-spirit, N815.0.2; sacred person, V206.

THE BUFFALO TUG-OF-WAR: Tale-Type No. 1271+; Motifs: speaking animals, B211; transformation by putting on skin, D531; deception into humiliating position, K1240+; deception by disguise, K1839.16; deception by substitution, K1840; deception punished, Q261+; miscellaneous punishments: drinking water forbidden, Q590; humor: lies about mammal, X1210+; trickster deceives the buffalo, Z209.2.1.

RABBIT AND THE TURKEYS: Tale-Type Nos. 1251+, 1353; Motifs: speaking animals, B211; gullible fools, J2349; trickster hoodwinks cook and eats food himself, K359+; birds enticed into a bag, K711.0.1; fatal deception into trickster's power, K839.9; deception by illusion, K1800; unfavorable character traits: selfishness, W150.

WHY RABBIT HAS BIG EYES AND LONG EARS: Tale-Type No. 1325+; Motifs: length of ears, A2325.1; size of eyes, A2332.3; speaking animals, B211; size of object transformed, D489.9; deceptive exchange, K140.1; deception in payment of debt, K200; deceptive bargain—bargain implicit, K250+.

RABBIT OUTWITS A FARMER: Tale-Type No. 1373+; Motifs: speaking animals, B211; unique prohibition, C640+; gullible fool, J2349; theft through alleged or deliberate or fabricated misunderstanding, K360+; death escaped through substitution, K527; deception into fatal substitution, K840; dupe's goods (axe) destroyed, K1410; deception by substitution, K1840; person unwittingly killed, N326; trickster outwits a farmer, Z209.2.2.

RABBIT PLAYS PRANKS ON BIG MAN-EATER: Tale-Type No. 972+; Motifs: speaking animals, B211; helpful animal, B301.9; magic power from animal, B500; animals save people's lives, B520+; elephants in folktales, B801; giant elephant, B871.2.1; river expands and becomes sea, D483.1; river magically widened, D2151.2.6; animal ogres with monstrous features, G360; animal ogre defeated, G580; separation of people and animal ogres by topographical feature, G650; escape from death or danger by deception, K500; victim trapped, K730; deception by mimicking shared injury with victim, K1110+; deception by illusion, K1800;

lies about plants and trees, X1400; lies about land features, X1510; trickster deceives an elephant, Z209.2.3.

THE TASKS OF RABBIT: Tale-Type No. 902+; Motifs: animal characteristics as reward, A2229.7; animal characteristics as punishment, A2239.11; miscellaneous causes of habits of animals, A2499.2; speaking animals, B211; action of animal community, B239.2; miscellaneous traits of animals, B799; transformation by putting on skin, D531; tasks imposed, H909; tasks performed through cleverness, H961; miscellaneous impossible tasks, H1049.5; tasks: slaying dangerous beasts, H1161.7; quest for dangerous animals, H1369; tests of power to survive, H1539; absurd attempt to change animal nature, J1908; capture (of wasps) by deception, K711.5; fatal deception into trickster's power, K839.9; murder by strategy, K929.14; deception by disguise, K1839.16; unfavorable character traits: bragging, deceitfulness, W199; miscellaneous lies and exaggerations, X1869; Achilles' heel, Z311.9.

THE BUNGLING HOST: Tale-Type No. 1210 J.1; Motifs: nose characteristics, A2335.2.6; speaking animals, B211; animal physician, B299.6; size of object transformed, D489.9; the bungling host—foolish imitation, J2425; sham doctor kills his patient, K824; deception through false doctoring, K1019; buzzard's sham prowess as physician, K1955.9.2; hypocrite pretends friendship but attacks, K2029; smoking as sign of sociability, P689; lie: occupational or professional skills, X1009.

OUTWITTING THE CANNIBALS: Tale-Type No. 981.1+; Motifs: creation of animals through transformation, A1715.6; creation of animals as punishment, A1739; creation of carnivora through transformation, A1839; creation of birds through transformation, A1999; creation of plants through transformation, A2611.0.5; unique prohibition, C640+; transformation: man to wild beast, D129; transformation: man to bird, D153.2; transformation through power of the word, D522; resuscitated girl, E1.9; resuscitation (of cannibal) by arrangement of members, E42.9; resuscitation by magic arrow, E61; severed head rejoins body, E783.2; extraordinary occurrence concerning water, F932.99; cannibalism, G19; bones of cannibal victim near a tree, G691.9; fatal deception into trickster's power, K839.9; murder of enemy's children, K939; absurdity based on the nature of the object (nose/pipe), X1789.

THE MAGIC FLIGHT: Tale-Type No. 982+; Motifs: creation of birds through transformation, A1999; creation of insects through transformation, A2001; helpful birds—general, B469; size of object transformed (plants, mud), D489.9; obstacle flight, D672; magic object a gift, D829.9; recovery of magic object, D899; magic plants, D965; magic fruits—general, D980+; magic berries, D981.10; magic object points out fugitive's route, D1313.19; magic object pursues, D1431.1; cannibalism, G19; the cannibal who was killed and burned, G512.19; help from cannibal's relative, G530.1; escape by making pursuit difficult, K639; capture by deception, K711.9; capture by decoy, K769; girl enticed into boat and abducted, R12.4; obstacle flight, R231; pursuit by rolling object, R261; mutilation of victim for cannibalism, S160.1; Achilles' heel, Z311.9.

THE GHOSTLY VISITANTS: Tale-Type No. 1048+; Motifs: glowing animals, B19.4; flying crustacean, B48; mythical beasts and hybrids, B94.9; revenant as owl, E423.3.5; animal ghosts, E522; phantom advisor, E599.14; spirit in animal form, F401.3; extraordinary occurrences concerning animals, F989.29; miscellaneous extraordinary events, F1099.9.

THE ALABAMAS CAPTURE A WITCH: Tale-Type No. 1048+; Motifs: characteristics of witches, G229.9; witch bathes with earth, G245.2; recognition of witches, G259.9; murderous witch, G260; witch snared, G274; witch executed for engaging in witchcraft, G291; witch must make amends for evil, G299.9; other deceptive captures, K789; murder by strategy, K929.14; capital punishment for witches, Q411.19.

HOW A HUNTER KILLED A GHOST: Tale-Type No. 1048+; Motifs: bloodthirsty revenants, E259.9; appearance of revenant, E422; ghosts placated by gift of food, E433.9; sun forces ghost to return to hiding place, E439.12; walking ghosts "laid," E446.2; escape, R219.9.

THE FLIGHT TO THE TREE: Tale-Type No. 511A+; Motifs: speaking animals, B211; marriage of person to animal, B601.19; buffalo as suitor, B621.9; magic object gives power over animals, D1449.9; magic egg straightens tree, saving orphan from buffalo, D1561.2; magic return of arrows, D1939; sleep induced by magic song, D1962; suitor test, H359.9; unpromising hero, L101, Z209.3; deeds rewarded, Q99; escape, R219.9; flights, R259; tree refuge, R311; murder, S110+.

A TRIP TO THE BEAD-SPITTER: Tale-Type No. 901D+; Motifs: mythical beasts and hybrids, B19.9; horned snake, B91.3; speaking animals, B211; speaking birds, B211.3; helpful animals, B301.9; helpful birds—general, B469; helpful crane, B463.3; animal carries man, B557.16; wild animals kept as dogs, B575.1; offspring of marriage to bird, B631.10; owl as suitor, B623.2; giant sea monster, 877.1; magic object gives power over animals, D1449.9; magic rejuvenation, D1887.1; sea animals magically called, D2074.1.2; dead animal comes to life, E3; resuscitated eaten animals, E32; water-spirit as snake, F420.1.3.9; extraordinary occurrences concerning animals, F989.29; inanimate object (pot) acts as if living, F1009.5; cannibalism, G19; identification by arrows, H125.5; suitor test: skill in hunt, H326.3; forethought in defense against other persons, J671; other deceptive captures, K789; murder by strategy, K914; woman wooed by trick, K1377; deception by disguise, K1839.16; deception by substitution, K1859; the false bridegroom, K1915; sham prowess: bead-spitter, K1969.5; helpful water-spirit, N815.0.2; rescue of captives, R129.

HOW THE ALABAMAS KILLED A MONSTER LIZARD: Tale-Type No. 972+; Motifs: giant lizard, B875.1; acquisition of magic powers, D1739.3; magic paralysis, D2039; lizard as ogre, G354.3; person falls into ogre's power, G405; capture by ogre, G429; ogre burned at his hiding place, G512.3.3; murder by strategy, K929.14;

life saved by accident, N659.3; escape, R219.9; flights, R259; tree refuge, R311.

THE BLACK PANTHER'S REQUEST: Tale-Type No. 972+; Motifs: speaking animal, B211; reward of helpful animal, B329; helpful panther, B431.4; animal rescuer, B544; animal carries man, B557.16; giant panther, B871.2.3; lizard as ogre, G354.3; capture by ogre, G429; ogre maimed, G510.6; rescue from ogre by helpful animal, G552; death escaped through shamming, K522; ogre carries sham-dead man, K522.2; deeds rewarded, Q99; reward: immunity from harm to selected animals, Q163; abduction by lizard, R13.4; rescue of captive, R129.

THE MONSTER DEER: Tale-Type No. 354+; Motifs: four cardinal directions, A1182+; creation of deer through transformation, A1724.2; origin of deer, A1875; attack on the giant deer, B16.2.7; speaking animal, B211; helpful squirrel, B437.3; helpful birds—general, B469; bird perched on deer, B853.1; giant deer, B871.3; transformation: hair to deer, D447.1.4; animal becomes larger, D487; magic results from special rituals, D1799.3; resuscitation by divine action, E121; friendly return from the dead, E390; extraordinary growth of animal, F983.5; animal ogre, G352.3; animal ogre subdued, G586; battle formation, P552; supernatural growth, T622; sacred person, V206.

THE MAN WITH HORNS: Tale-Type No. 1048+; Motifs: miraculous growth of hero, A511.4.2; magic changes in man himself, D55; person becomes larger, D486; magic object otherwise obtained (wolf's head), D859.9; magic horns grow on person's forehead, D992.1; magic animal head, D1011; magic object gives supernatural information, D1310.2; cut-off head prophesies fight, D1311.8.2; person with horns, F511.0.9.4; exceptionally large man, F534; horns on forehead, F545.2.2; extraordinary powers of perception, F645; favorable prophecies, M323; unfavorable prophecies, M340.5; supernatural helpers, N819.5; care of children, T606; supernatural growth of hero, T623; Horned Man assists Alabamas, Z209.4.

LODGE BOY AND LOST BOY: Tale-Type No. 1101+; Motifs: tabu: contact with supernatural, C99.3; tabu: doing deed of mercy, C748; magic adhesion to monster, D2171.2; house-spirit accidentally acquired, F481.0.1.4; difficult to rid oneself of house-spirit, F481.3.1; pestilence in human form, F493.0.2; burr-man: old man of the sea, G311; rescue from ogre, G557; deception by disguise, K1839.16; shooting contest on wager, N55; Lodge-Boy and Thrown-Away, Z210.1.

THE DIRTY BOY: Tale-Type No. 922+; Motifs: bird characteristics: color, A2411.2.5.4; speaking animal, B211; loathly bridegroom, D733; magic objects acquired by trickery, D838; magic headdress; D1079.4; magic flute, D1223.1; other permanent magic characteristics (attracting fish, etc.), D1937; other remarkable powers, F699.2; absurd disregard of natural laws, J1959.3; fatal imitation, J2401; imitation of magic rejuvenation unsuccessful, J2411.1; unsuccessful imitation of magic production of food, J2411.3; bungling fool, J2690; means of hoodwinking owner, K341.4.2; escape by deceiving the guard, K629.3; dupe tricked into killing himself, K899; treacherous impostor, K1946; unpromising hero given great powers by deity, L103; success of the unpromising hero, L179; overweening ambition punished, L428; animal eludes bird watchman and escapes from his hole, R214; boy reared in ignorance of world, T617; unpromising hero, Z209.3.

THE PIGEON HAWK'S GIFT: Tale-Type No. 1112+; Motifs: speaking birds, B211.3; magic sabia, D1299.6; means of producing magic power, D1799.7; defense against spirits, E439.11; success of the unpromising hero, L179; protection rewarded, Q96; punishment fitted to crime, Q582.10; unpromising hero, Z209.3.

THE ALABAMA AND CHOCTAW WARS: Local legend; motifs were not catalogued.

THE ALABAMAS TRAVEL WESTWARD: Local legend; motifs were not catalogued.

CHIEF COLITA OF THE COUSHATTA INDIANS: Local legend; motifs were not catalogued.

THE PYGMIES: Tale-Type No. 1048+; Motifs: tree spirits—tiny, F441.5.1; pygmies: exceptionally small men, F535; war of pygmies and yellow jackets, F535.5.1.2; adventures of extraordinary companions, F601.8; extraordinarily small weapons, F839.8; help from little men, N821; favorable traits of character: cooperation, W46.

THE MAN WHO BECAME A SNAKE: Tale-Type No. 354+; Motifs: catfish with unusual coloring, B731.0.2; tabu: eating certain fish, C221.1.3.1; transformation: man to snake, D191; transformation by breaking tabu, D519; transformation by eating fish, D551.3.1; magic meal of fish, D1032.1.

THE ESCAPE FROM AN EAGLE: Tale-Type No. 971+; Motifs: man-eating birds, B33; eagle forced to carry man to safety, B542.1.1; eagle carries man, B552; giant eagle, B872.1; eagle carries off youth, R13.3.2; man captured as food for eaglets, R65; escape from nest of eagle, R219.3; escape from eagle's nest by riding eagle to the ground, R253.1, Z209.5.

ABA MIKKO'S SON AND THE CORN GRINDER: Tale-Type No. 292+; Motifs: Creator's advisers, A42.3; action of Creator in restoring peace, A88; God in relation to mortals, A185.15.1; beginnings of trouble for man, A1342; development of social relationships, A1470+; soul leaves body at death, E722; inhabitant of other world visits earth, F36; access to other world, F50+; spirits (general), F419; dead remain standing, F1041.25; the deceived blind man (blind dupe), K331.1.1; man deceived into killing another person, K929.7.1; treacherous murder, K959.7; trouble-makers, K2130; innocent made to appear guilty, K2150; person unwittingly killed, N326; supernatural helper comes from sky, N810.4; friendship as divine dictum, P319.9; sacred person, V206; miracle manifested, V348.

Glossary

ABA MIKKO: God, Creator. "Aba" means "above" in the languages of several Indian tribes in the southeastern region of the United States. The Alabama word for chief is "Micco" or "Mikko."

ALABAMA TRIBE: In 1921 Dr. T. M. Owen, Director of the Alabama State Department of Archives and History, summarized several studies relating to the etymology of "Alabama," by pointing out that it is a derivation of Choctaw words— "alba" (vegetation) and "amo" (to gather). Dr. Owen suggests that "vegetation gatherers" more accurately identifies the Alabama tribe of Indians because, in their aboriginal field-making, they were necessarily "thicket clearers." (Thomas McAdory Owen, *History of Alabama and Dictionary of Alabama Biography*, Chicago: S. J. Clarke Publishing Co., 1921, I, 15-16.)

BERDACHE: A man who was believed to be directed by the moon, a female spirit, to dress as a woman and perform women's tasks. A berdache had the ability to foretell future events, and was at one time a highly honored and respected person.

BIG MAN-EATER: Alabamas and Coushattas in the twentieth century identify Big Man-Eaters as elephants. The conception of a flesh-eating monster is probably a mythical rationalization based on observation of the remains of mastodons and other large creatures scattered abundantly over the United States.

BLOWGUN: A cane tube from which darts are propelled by the breath. Alabamas and Coushattas used tubular cane blowguns to kill small animals and birds. This weapon was made from a straight cane, 8 to 10 feet in length. The cane was bored by using a wooden or iron rod to break through the segment barriers. The outside was scraped to smooth the joints, and was polished by rubbing. Arrows for blowguns usually were made of cane slivers about 10 inches in length and round in cross section. The piston end or plunger was formed with down from bull thistle, chicken feathers, or cotton. The effective range of this weapon was approximately 50 feet.

CABIN: The Alabamas and Coushattas usually constructed their cabins of pine logs. A cabin was rectangular in ground plan, had a gable roof, and was located in relation to prevailing winds. Two smoke-holes or vents, one at the top of each gable-end, served for the admission of fresh air and the expulsion of smoke, since these Indians made fires in the middle of the cabins.

CARDINAL POINTS: The conception of the four world-quarters is a fundamental idea expressed in the actions of various characters in Alabama-Coushatta narratives. For example, in "How Fire Came to the Alabamas and Coushattas," the fire rescuers picked up sticks from each of the cardinal directions—north, west, south, and east—to revive the dying fire. Also, the village square-ground was designed so that each side faced a cardinal point. The rankings of groups within the village social structure was related to the four principal points of the compass, since each group was assigned seats on a side of the square-ground in accordance with the group's significance in the community.

CHOCTAW TRIBE: This was the largest tribe belonging to the southern Muskhogean branch. Most of the Choctaws lived in Mississippi, but tribal control was extended eastward to the Tombigbee River in Alabama. For most of its length, the Tombigbee River served as the boundary between the Choctaws and the tribes of the Creek Confederacy. In the eighteenth century the Choctaws were almost constantly at war with the Alabamas and Coushattas.

CHUNK STONE: This rolling or hurling stone, about three inches in diameter, was used in the chungke or chunkey game. Each stone was rubbed smooth on rocks, preserved very carefully, and passed from one generation to another. In Alabama-Coushatta narratives this stone was spoken of as if it had human characteristics. Monsters trailed their intended victims by means of chunk stones, which also are referred to as magic rollers.

COUSHATTA TRIBE: The popular form of the name of this tribe is Coushatta, but Bureau of American Ethnology publications use Koasati. In *The Handbook of the American Indians,* the editor, Dr. F. W. Hodge, points out that the name "Koasati" probably contains the word for "cane" or "reed," and Dr. Albert S. Gatschet has suggested that it might signify "white cane." (F. W. Hodge, *Handbook of the American Indians,* Washington, D. C.: U. S. Government Printing Office, 1912, Bureau of American Ethnology Bulletin 30, 719-720.)

HORNED OWL-CRAWFISH: A mythical hybrid; a flying crustacean.

HORNED SNAKE: This mythical hybrid also is referred to as a snake-crawfish and a water-spirit. It lived in water and had horns that were valued as hunting charms. These horns varied in color—yellow, white, red, or blue—among these awesome creatures, and small pieces of the horns brought good luck in hunting and killing deer.

KOASATI: (see Coushatta).

LITTLE PEOPLE: (see Pygmies).

LODGE: (see Cabin).

MAGIC ROLLER: (see Chunk stone).

MONSTER LIZARD: This very large animal resembled, except for size, the small, inoffensive lizard usually found on shrubbery and trees. The monster lizard lived like a bear in hollow trees.

MOTIF: In *The Folktale,* Dr. Stith Thompson differentiated between tale-type and motif. He pointed out that a tale-type is a traditional tale that has an independent existence and may be told as a complete narrative. A motif, according to Dr. Thompson, is the smallest element in a tale having the potential to persist in tradition. The three types of motifs which he listed include the actors in a tale, certain items in the background of the action, and single incidents. (Stith Thompson, *The Folktale,* New York: The Dryden Press, 1946, 415-416.)

OWL-CRAWFISH: (see Horned Owl-Crawfish).

PYGMIES: The mythical supernatural beings mentioned in the narratives of this collection include a race of pygmies, or little people, the term that still is used by residents of the Alabama-Coushatta Reservation in referring to these small persons. Most of the little people lived in hollow trees; the others lived in tree tops or in caves. Human beings contacted by the little people occasionally developed a mental disease which left the victims in a state of bewilderment or temporary insanity.

ROLLER: (see Chunk stone).

SABIA: Among the charms used to secure supernatural help, the sabia was the most important. It was a small crystalline object resembling a glass bead, which, when properly handled, would bring the owner success in various activities. The colors of the sabia included white, blue, red, yellow, and black. The sabia was kept in a piece of buckskin along with red paint. When the owner wanted to improve his luck while hunting, for example, he unwrapped the sabia, took out a little red paint with a stick, and put the paint on his cheek—an action that transmitted the power of the sabia to the hunter.

SMOKE-HOLE: (see Cabin).

SNAKE-CRAWFISH: (see Horned Snake).

SPUNK: Tinder made from woody material or from various fungi.

SQUARE-GROUND: Each village or community of the Alabamas and Coushattas was organized around a central ceremonial area or square-ground—a typical arrangement among tribes of the Creek Confederacy. On the four sides of this square, which faced the four cardinal points of the compass, lodges or cabins with brush-covered roofs were erected. Of the buildings or sheds constructed on the sides of the square-ground, the first in rank was the chief's or mikko's cabin, which was located on the east side. Split logs, laid with flat sides uppermost and arranged around the square, served as seats. Villagers were assigned places at the square-ground in order of rank. Council meetings, ceremonies, dances, and other types of public activities were held on the square-ground.

SWEAT-HOUSE: The sweat-house or sweat-lodge was a universal institution among North American Indians. Nearly all tribes of the southeastern United States used sweat baths to enhance supernatural powers and to cure the sick.

A sweat-house was usually a small lodge constructed of skins or blankets thrown over a framework of poles. Red-hot stones were placed in the center of the sweat-house, and from time to time water was thrown over the stones to generate heat and steam. Persons using a sweat-house usually stayed in the heated enclosure about 30 minutes and then would depart to dive into the nearest water, preferably a cold stream.

Before going on a hunting trip, Alabamas and Coushattas steamed themselves in a sweat-house and then plunged into a cold stream—for the purpose of improving their luck while hunting. Also, during hunting trips they put Indian tobacco under every campfire to keep away the maleficent spirits of the dead.

TALE-TYPE: (see Motif).

TIE SNAKE: This snake is said to have originated from a transformed human being. In the *Forty-Second Annual Report of the Bureau of American Ethnology*, Dr. John R. Swanton reported the following description of this snake: "The 'tie snake' is an inch and a half in diameter and short, but it is very strong. It is white under the throat, but black over the rest of the body, and its head is crooked over like the beak of a hawk. It lives in deep water, usually in small deep water holes from which it makes excursions into the woods, drawing its prey down into the water to its den." (John R. Swanton, "Social Organization and Social Usages of the Creek Confederacy," *Forty-Second Annual Report of the Bureau of American Ethnology, 1924-1925*, Washington, D.C.: U. S. Government Printing Office, 1928, 492.)

TOMBIGBEE RIVER: This river is located in western Alabama. In the eighteenth century the Tombigbee served as an important part of the boundary between the Choctaws and the tribes of the Creek Confederacy.

VILLAGE: Alabama and Coushatta villages were not compact settlements. Typically, a community established by one of these tribes consisted of a square-ground and a succession of neighborhoods scattered for miles through the woods and connected by a network of trails—a pattern which may be observed on the present Alabama-Coushatta Reservation.

WATER-SPIRIT: (see Horned Snake).

Selected Reading References

Bascom, William R. "Four Functions of Folklore." *Journal of American Folklore,* 67 (1954): 333-349.

———. "The Forms of Folklore: Prose Narratives." *Journal of American Folklore,* 78 (1965): 3-20.

Boas, Franz. *The Mind of Primitive Man.* 1911. Revised Edition. New York: The Free Press, 1966.

———. "Religion." In *Handbook of American Indians North of Mexico,* Part 2, edited by Frederick Webb Hodge, pp. 365-371. Washington, D.C.: Government Printing Office, 1912.

———. "Mythology and Folk-Tales of the North American Indians." *Journal of American Folk-Lore,* 27 (1914): 404-410.

———. "The Development of Folk-Tales and Myths." *The Scientific Monthly,* 3 (1916): 335-343.

———. *Race, Language, and Culture.* New York: The Macmillan Company, 1940.

Bushnell, David I., Jr. "Myths of the Louisiana Choctaw." *American Anthropologist,* 12 (new series, 1910): 526-535.

———. *Native Villages and Village Sites East of the Mississippi,* Bureau of American Ethnology, Bulletin 69, Washington, D.C.: Government Printing Office, 1919.

Campbell, T. N. "The Choctaw Afterworld." *Journal of American Folklore,* 72 (1959): 146-154.

Culin, Stewart. "American Indian Games." *American Anthropologist,* 5 (1903): 58-64.

Dixon, R. B. "Culture Contact and Migration versus Independent Origin: A Plea for More Light." *American Anthropologist,* 20 (new series, 1918): 124-128.

Dorson, Richard M. "A Theory for American Folklore." *Journal of American Folklore,* 72 (1959): 197-215.

Folsom-Dickerson, W. E. S. *The White Path.* San Antonio: The Naylor Company, 1965.

Freeman, Theresa J. "Early Discoveries of the Mastodon." *American Antiquarian and Oriental Journal,* 23 (1901): 320-322.

Gatschet, Albert S. "Some Mythic Stories of the Yuchi Indians." *American Anthropologist,* 6 (1893): 279-282.

———. "The Whip-Poor-Will as Named in American Languages." *American Antiquarian and Oriental Journal,* 18 (1896): 39-42.

Gotesky, Rubin. "The Nature of Myth and Society." *American Anthropologist,* 54 (1952): 523-531.

Halbert, H. S. "Pits and Ambushes." *American Antiquarian and Oriental Journal,* 5 (1883): 277-278.

_____. "The Derivation of Mobile and Alabama." *American Antiquarian and Oriental Journal,* 23 (1901): 178.

Hallowell, A. Irving. "The Impact of the American Indian on American Culture." *American Anthropologist,* 59 (1957): 201-217.

Hodge, Frederick Webb, ed. *Handbook of American Indians North of Mexico,* Bureau of American Ethnology, Bulletin 30. 2 vols. Washington, D.C.: Government Printing Office, 1912.

Klapp, Orrin E. "The Folk Hero." *Journal of American Folklore,* 62 (1949): 17-25.

_____. "The Clever Hero." *Journal of American Folklore,* 67 (1954): 21-34.

Kluckhohn, Clyde. "Myths and Rituals: A General Theory." *Harvard Theological Review,* 35 (1942): 45-79.

_____. "Recurrent Themes in Myths and Mythmaking." In *Myth and Mythmaking,* edited by Henry A. Murray. 1960. Reprint. Boston: Beacon Press, 1968.

Lamb, D. S. "Mythical Monsters." *American Anthropologist,* 2 (new series, 1900): 277-291.

Lang, Andrew. *Myth, Ritual, and Religion.* 2 vols. London, New York, and Bombay: Longmans, Green & Co., 1906.

Littleton, C. Scott. "A Two-Dimensional Scheme for the Classification of Narratives." *Journal of American Folklore,* 78 (1965): 21-27.

Lowie, Robert H. "The Test-Theme in North American Mythology." *Journal of American Folk-Lore,* 21 (1908): 97-147.

_____. *Primitive Religion.* 1924. Reprint. New York: Grosset & Dunlap, Inc., 1948.

Mooney, James. "Myths of the Cherokee." In *Nineteenth Annual Report of the Bureau of American Ethnology, 1897-98,* Part 1, edited by J. W. Powell. Washington, D.C.: Government Printing Office, 1900.

Moore, Remedios Wycoco. "The Types of North-American Indian Tales." Unpublished Ph.D. dissertation, Indiana University, 1951.

Nida, Eugene A., and Smalley, William A. *Introducing Animism.* New York: Friendship Press, 1959.

Owen, Thomas McAdory. *History of Alabama and Dictionary of Alabama Biography.* Vol. 1. Chicago: S. J. Clarke Publishing Co., 1921.

Peet, Stephen D. "The Mound-Builders and the Mastodon." *American Antiquarian and Oriental Journal,* 13 (1891): 59-81.

_____. "The Story of the Creation Among the American Aborigines: A Proof of Prehistoric Contact." *American Antiquarian and Oriental Journal,* 17 (1895): 127-150.

Powell, J. W. *Outlines of the Philosophy of the North American Indians.* New York: Douglas Taylor, Printer, 1877.

_____. "The Lessons of Folklore." *American Anthropologist,* 2 (new series, 1900): 1-36.

Radin, Paul. "Religion of the North American Indians." *Journal of American Folk-Lore,* 27 (1914): 335-373.

_____. *Primitive Religion: Its Nature and Origin.* 1937. Reprint. New York: Dover Publications, Inc., 1957.

Rands, Robert L., and Riley, Carroll L. "Diffusion and Discontinuous Distribution." *American Anthropologist,* 60 (1958): 274-297.

Reichard, Gladys A. "Literary Types and Dissemination of Myths." *Journal of American Folk-Lore,* 34 (1921): 269-307.

Rooth, Anna Birgitta. "The Creation Myths of the North American Indians." *Anthropos,* 52 (1957): 497-508.

Schoolcraft, Henry Rowe. *Algic Researches: Indian Tales and Legends.* Vol. 1. New York: Harper & Brothers, 1839.

Smither, Harriet. "The Alabama Indians of Texas." *Southwestern Historical Quarterly,* 36 (1932): 83-108.

Speck, Frank C. "Some Outlines of Aboriginal Culture in the Southeastern States." *American Anthropologist,* 9 (new series, 1907): 287-295.

_____. "The Cane Blowgun in Catawba and Southeastern Ethnology." *American Anthropologist,* 40 (1938): 198-204.

Strong, W. D. "North American Indian Traditions Suggesting a Knowledge of the Mammoth." *American Anthropologist,* 36 (new series, 1934): 81-88.

Swanton, John R. "Some Practical Aspects of the Study of Myths." *Journal of American Folk-Lore,* 23 (1910): 1-7.

_____. "Results of Some Recent Investigations Regarding the Southeastern Tribes of the United States." *American Anthropologist,* 15 (new series, 1913): 690-691.

_____. "Animal Stories from the Indians of the Muskhogean Stock." *Journal of American Folk-Lore,* 26 (1913): 193-218.

_____. "An Early Account of the Choctaw Indians." *Memoirs of the American Anthropological Association,* 5 (1918): 53-72.

_____. *Early History of the Creek Indians and Their Neighbors,* Bureau of American Ethnology, Bulletin 73. Washington, D.C.: Government Printing Office, 1922.

_____. "Social Organization and Social Usages of the Indians of the Creek Confederacy." In *Forty-Second Annual Report of the Bureau of American Ethnology, 1924-1925,* pp. 23-472. Washington, D.C.: Government Printing Office, 1928.

_____. "Religious Beliefs and Medical Practices of the Creek Indians." In *Forty-Second Annual Report of the Bureau of American Ethnology, 1924-1925,* pp. 473-672. Washington, D.C.: Government Printing Office, 1928.

_____. "Aboriginal Culture of the Southeast." In *Forty-Second Annual Report of the Bureau of American Ethnology, 1924-1925,* pp. 673-726. Washington, D.C.: Government Printing Office, 1928.

_____. *Myths and Tales of the Southeastern Indians,* Bureau of American Ethnology, Bulletin 88. Washington, D.C.: Government Printing Office, 1929.

_____. "Notes on the Cultural Province of the Southeast." *American Anthropologist,* 37 (1935): 373-385.

——. *The Indians of the Southeastern United States*, Bureau of American Ethnology, Bulletin 137. Washington, D.C.: Government Printing Office, 1946.

——. *The Indian Tribes of North America*, Bureau of American Ethnology, Bulletin 145. Washington, D.C.: Government Printing Office, 1953.

Thompson, Stith. *Tales of the North American Indians*. Cambridge, Mass.: Harvard University Press, 1929.

——. *The Folktale*. New York: The Dryden Press, 1946.

——. "Myths and Folktales." *Journal of American Folklore*, 68 (1955): 482-488.

——. *Motif-Index of Folk-Literature*. Revised Edition. Bloomington: Indiana University Press, 1955-1958.

Tylor, Edward Burnett. *The Origins of Culture*. Part 1 of *Primitive Culture*, 1871. Reprint. New York: Harper & Row, Publishers, Inc., 1958.

——. *Religion in Primitive Culture*. Part 2 of *Primitive Culture*, 1871. Reprint. New York: Harper & Row, Publishers, Inc., 1958.

Ullom, Judith C. *Folklore of the North American Indians*. Washington, D. C.: Government Printing Office, 1969.

Warner, H. E. "The Magic Flight in Folk-Lore." *Scribner's Magazine*, 1 (1887): 762-766.

Waterman, T. T. "The Explanatory Element in the Folk-Tales of the North-American Indians." *Journal of American Folk-Lore*, 27 (1914): 1-54.

——. "The Architecture of the American Indians." *American Anthropologist*, 29 (new series, 1927): 210-230.

Wheeler-Voegelin, Erminie, and Moore, Remedios Wycoco. "The Emergence Myth in Native North America." In *Studies in Folklore*, edited by W. Edson Richmond, pp. 66-91. Bloomington: Indiana University Press, 1957.

Wilson, Eddie W. "The Owl and the American Indian." *Journal of American Folklore*, 63 (1950): 336-344.

Wycoco (Moore), Remedios. "The Types of North-American Indian Tales." Unpublished Ph.D. dissertation, Indiana University, 1951.

Index

Motifs in the Alabama-Coushatta myths and folktales are listed in the appendix.

69, 76-78, 97, 98, 100
Christianity, xxii
Chunk stone, 46, 47, 58, 98
Civil War service, xx, xxi
Clay as origin of Alabamas and
    Coushattas, xxx, 3
Clay bowl, 68; bucket, 56; pot, 6, 8, 9,
    59
Clothing, 12
Club, 45
Colita, xix, xx, xxxv, 79, 80, 81
Colita's Village, xix, xx
Color (feathers), 10
Color (in blankets), 12
Comanche tribe, xxi
Combat, earth and sky, 26
Compass-oriented, 65, 99
Compass, principal points of, 98
Confederate military service, xx, xxi
Conflict, 25, 26
Contest, strength, 30
Cook, 44
Coosa River, xvii
Corn cultivation, 5
Corn-grinders, 86, 87
Corn pounding, 60
Corn storage, 5
Cosmic creative agencies, xxviii
Cosmogony, xxvii
Cosmology, xxvii
Council, 2, 6, 8, 12, 13, 17, 19, 20,
    35, 37, 51, 86
Coushatta etymology, xvii
Coushatta population, xix, xx
Coushatta Trace, xviii, xix
Coushatta tribe, xvii-xix, xxiii-xxv,
    xxx, xxxii, xxxv, 3, 7, 12, 65,
    80, 81, 98-100
Coushatta villages, in Alabama, xviii;
    in Louisiana, xviii; in Texas, xviii-
    xx, xxxv
Crane, 18, 59, 73

Crawfish, xxvi, xxvii, 2, 3
Creation, myths about, xxvii, xxviii,
    xxix
Creative agencies, cosmic, xxviii
Creek Confederacy, xvii, xxxv, 98-
    100
Cricket, 15
Crippled man, 70
Crow, 18
Crustacean, flying, 98
Cultural diffusion of tale elements,
    xxiv, xxv, xxvii, xxxi
Dance, 16, 32, 57
Dancer, 6
Decline in Texas, xxi
Deer, xxix, xxxiii, 16, 52, 58, 64,
    65, 69, 73, 74, 77, 79
Deer hide, 7
Deerskin, 17, 31, 53; bags, 24, 31;
    cords, 72; shirt, 77; wrapping, 15
Deluge, xxviii, 9
Densmore, Frances, x
DeSoto, Hernando, xvii
Diffusion, cultural, of tale elements,
    xxiv, xxv, xxvii, xxxi
Dobie, J. Frank, xii, xiii
Doctor, 40
Dogs, 34, 58, 63, 73
Domed sky, xxvii, xxviii, xxx
Domed vault, xxvii, xxviii
Drooling, 16
Dual afterworld, xxix, xxx
Ducks, 17
Dupe, blind, xxxv
Eagle, xxx, xxxv, 12, 24, 85, 86
Eaglets, 86
Ears lengthened, 33
Earth, 26; Alabama-Coushatta con-
    ception of, xxvii, xxviii; creation
    of, xxvii
Earth-diver, xxvii
Earth's edge, 26

Magic pot, 5
Magic power, xxxii
Magic rain, 76
Magic roller, 46, 47, 98
Magic sabia, 74
Magic song, 36, 56
Magic words, 45
Man-Eater, Big, xxxiii, 35, 36, 97
Man vis-a-vis environment, xxxii
Marriage, humans and animals, xxxii,
    xxxiii
Mastodons, 97
Measurement, 37
Medicine, 40, 65
Medicine men, xxxii, 65
Mexican Army, 80
Mexicans, 79-81
Mexico, xxxv, 79
Middle Coushatta Village, xix
Migration westward, ix, xvii, xviii,
    xxxv, 24
Mikko, 97, 99
Minnow, 73
Miracle, 87
Mississippi, state, xvii, 98
Mobile, Alabama, xvii
Mobile, tribe, xvii
Moccasins, 32, 33, 74, 77
Monster deer, 65
Monster lizard, 62-64, 98
Monster stories, origin, xxxiii
Monsters, xxxiii, xxxiv, 62-64;
    storytelling mechanisms, xxxiii,
    xxxiv
Montgomery, Alabama, xvii
Montgomery County, Texas, 79;
    settlers, 80
Months, division among birds and ani-
    mals, 4
Moon, exchange with sun, 4
Mooney, James, xxix, xxxvi, xxxvii
Mosquitoes, 24, 47

Moss, 12; blankets, 12; strands, 13
Motif, 98
Motif dissemination, xxxi
Motifs, mythological, xxviii
Mountains, 24, 85, 86
Mud, xxxi, 46, 47
Mud chimney, 2
Murder, 57, 58
Murrah, Governor Pendleton, xx
Muskhogean, xvii, 98
Muskogee, xvii
Myth, xxiii
Mythical hybrid, 98
Mythological incidents, xxvii, xxviii
Mythological motifs, xxviii
Nacogdoches, Texas, xviii
Narratives, categories, xxvi, xxvii;
    prose, xxiii; sections, xxvi, xxvii
Natchitoches, Louisiana, xviii
Neches River, xviii, xix, 79
Neutrality (in Texas War for Indepen-
    dence), xix
Noah, xxviii
Noises, weird, 50
North America, xxxi
Nostrils, enlargement, 40, 41
Number (of repetitions, occurrences,
    objects), xxvi, xxvii
Oak trees, 80
Ocean, 2, 18, 25, 34, 36, 58, 59; pri-
    meval, xxvi-xxviii
Ogre, xxxi
Old Man, 70-71
Opelousas, Louisiana, xviii, xix, 78
Opossum, 15, 16, 19, 20
Origins, myths about, xxvii-xxx
Orphan, xxvi, 16-18, 40, 44, 56, 57,
    71-73
Owen, Thomas McAdory, 97
Owl, xxxiii, 2, 3, 45, 51, 57, 58, 60,
    74
Oxen, 78

Index   113